William Fearing Gill

Golden Treasures of Poetry, Romance, and Art

William Fearing Gill

Golden Treasures of Poetry, Romance, and Art

ISBN/EAN: 9783337048624

Printed in Europe, USA, Canada, Australia, Japan

Cover: Foto ©Thomas Meinert / pixelio.de

More available books at **www.hansebooks.com**

LISTENING TO THE NEW YEAR'S CHIMES.

Golden Treasures

OF

POETRY, ROMANCE, AND ART

BY

EMINENT POETS, NOVELISTS, AND ESSAYISTS

Illustrated

BOSTON
WILLIAM F. GILL AND COMPANY
309 WASHINGTON STREET

1876

PREFACE.

HE demand for a volume which should combine the rarest products of the pictorial art with literary attractions of a high order of excellence, has not often been met, of late years, in illustrated works for mature readers. "GOLDEN TREASURES" presents what it is hoped will be found a happy combination of these sterling features.

It includes the freshest writings of contemporaneous authors with a leaven of gems by standard writers, and, pictorially, presents many artistic reproductions of beautiful works of art, otherwise unattainable except in a very costly form.

Acknowledgments are especially due to the prominent American authors represented in the volume, for their courtesy in permitting the use of selections from their most recent writings.

GOLDEN

TREASURES.

POETRY,

ROMANCE

AND

ART.

CONTENTS

CONTENTS.

LIST OF ILLUSTRATIONS

Engraved by F. Juengling, John Andrew & Son, Russell and Richardson, and J. S. Conant.

PRINTED BY THE ART PRINTING CO., NO. 30 BOND STREET, NEW YORK.

NEW YEAR'S MORNING.

NEW YEAR'S MORNING.

BY H. H.

NLY a night from Old to New!
Only a night — and so much wrought!
The Old Year's heart all weary grew,
But said, "The New Year rest has brought."
The Old Year's heart its hopes laid down,
As in a grave; but, trusting, said,
"The blossoms of the New Year's crown
Bloom from the ashes of the dead."
The old Year's heart was full of greed;
With selfishness it longed and ached,
And cried, "I have not half I need.
My thirst is bitter and unslaked.
But to the New Year's generous hand
All gifts in plenty shall return;
True loving, it shall understand,
By all my failures it shall learn.
I have been reckless : it shall be
Quiet and calm and pure of life.
I was a slave : it shall go free,
And find sweet peace where I leave strife."

Only a night from Old to New!
Never a night such changes brought.
The Old Year had its work to do;
No New Year miracles are wrought.

Always a night from old to new!
Night and the healing balm of sleep!
Each morn is New Year's morn come true,
Morn of a festival to keep.
All nights are sacred nights to make
Confession and resolve and prayer;

All days are sacred days to wake
New gladness in the sunny air.
Only a night from old to new;
Only a sleep from night to morn.
The new is but the old come true;
Each sunrise sees a new year born!

INCOMPLETENESS.

INCOMPLETENESS.

By ADELAIDE A. PROCTER.

OTHING resting in its own completeness
Can have worth or beauty; but alone
Because it leads and tends to further sweetness,
Fuller, higher, deeper than its own.

Spring's real glory dwells not in the meaning,
Gracious though it be, of her blue hours;
But is hidden in her tender leaning
To the Summer's richer wealth of flowers.

INCOMPLETENESS.

Dawn is fair because the mists fade slowly
   Into day, which floods the world with light :
Twilight's mystery is so sweet and holy,
   Just because it ends in starry night.

Childhood's smiles unconscious graces borrow
   From strife that in a far-off future lies ;
And angel glances (veiled now by life's sorrow)
   Draw our hearts to some beloved eyes.

Life is only bright when it proceedeth
   Towards a truer, deeper life above ;
Human love is sweetest when it leadeth
   To a more divine and perfect love.

Learn the mystery of progression duly,
   Do not call each glorious change decay ;
But know we only hold our treasures truly
   When it seems as if they had passed away :

Nor dare to blame God's gifts for incompleteness :
   In that want their beauty lies ; they roll
Towards some infinite depth of love and sweetness,
   Bearing onward man's reluctant soul.

LITTLE STREAMS.

LITTLE STREAMS.

BY MARY HOWITT.

ITTLE streams are light and shadow ;
Flowing through the pasture meadow,
Flowing by the green way-side,
Through the forest dim and wide,
Through the hamlet still and small —
By the cottage, by the hall,
By the ruin'd abbey still ;
Turning here and there a mill,
Bearing tribute to the river —
Little streams, I love you ever.

Summer music is there flowing —
Flowering plants in them are growing ;
Happy life is in them all,
Creatures innocent and small ;
Little birds come down to drink ;
Fearless of their leafy brink ;
Noble trees beside them grow,
Glooming them with branches low ;
And between, the sunshine, glancing
In their little waves, is dancing.

Down in valleys green and lowly,
Murmuring not and gliding slowly ;
Up in mountain-hollows wild,
Fretting like a peevish child :
Through the hamlet, where all day
In their waves the children play ;
Running west or running east,
Doing good to man and beast —
Always giving, weary never,
Little streams, I love you ever.

SONNET.

SONNET.

BY JAMES RUSSELL LOWELL.

The little bird sits at his door in the sun,
  Atilt like a blossom among the leaves,
And lets his illumined being o'errun
  With the deluge of summer it receives;
His mate feels the eggs beneath her wings,
And the heart in her dumb breast flutters and sings;
  He sings to the wide world, and she to her nest, —
In the nice ear of Nature, which song is the best?

THE
CLERGYMAN'S CONFESSION.

THE CLERGYMAN'S CONFESSION.

BY WILKIE COLLINS.

PART FIRST.

I.

M Y BROTHER, the clergyman, looked over my shoulder before I was aware of him, and discovered that the volume which completely absorbed my attention was a collection of famous trials, published in a new edition and in a popular form. He laid his finger on the trial which I happened to be reading at the moment. I looked up at him ; his face startled me. He had turned pale. His eyes were fixed on the open page of the book with an expression which puzzled and alarmed me.

"My dear fellow," I said, "what in the world is the matter with you?"

He answered in an odd, absent manner, still keeping his finger on the open page.

"I had almost forgotten," he said, "and this reminds me."

"Reminds you of what?" I asked. "You don't mean to say you know anything about the trial?"

"I know this," he said: "the prisoner was guilty."

"Guilty?" I repeated. "Why, the man was acquitted by the jury, with the full approval of the judge! What can you possibly mean?"

"There are circumstances connected with that trial," my

brother answered, "which were never communicated to the judge or the jury—which were never so much as hinted or whispered in court. *I* know them of my own knowledge—by my own personal experience. They are very sad, very strange, very terrible. I have mentioned them to no mortal creature. I have done my best to forget them. You, quite innocently, have brought them back to my mind. They oppress, they distress me. I wish I had found you reading any book in your library, except *that* book!"

My curiosity was now strongly excited. I spoke out plainly.

"Might it not relieve your mind," I suggested, "if you admitted some one into your confidence? You might surely tell your brother what you are unwilling to mention to persons less nearly related to you. We have followed different professions, and have lived in different countries, since we were boys at school. But you know you can trust me."

He considered a little with himself.

"Yes," he said, "I know I can trust you." He waited a moment, and then he surprised me by a strange question.

"Do you believe," he asked, "that the spirits of the dead can return to earth, and show themselves to the living?"

I answered cautiously, adopting as my own the words of a great English writer, touching the subject of ghosts.

"You ask me a question," I said, "which, after five thousand years, is yet undecided. On that account alone it is a question not to be trifled with."

My reply seemed to satisfy him.

"You suggested just now," he resumed, "that it might relieve my mind if I took you into my confidence. You may be right; and, as my nearest living relative, you are certainly the fittest person whom I can trust. Promise me that you will keep what I tell you a secret as long as I live. After my death I care little what happens. Let the story of my strange experience be added to the published experience of those other men who have seen what I have seen, and who believe what I believe. The world will not be the worse, and may be the better, for knowing one day what I am now about to confide to your ear alone."

He began his narrative, as nearly as I can remember, in these words : —

II.

On a fine summer evening, many years since, I left my chambers in the Temple, to meet a fellow-student who had proposed to me a night's amusement in the public gardens at Cremorne.

You had then gone out to India, and I had just taken my degree at Oxford. I had sadly disappointed my father by choosing the law as my profession, in preference to the Church. At that time, to own the truth, I had no serious intention of following any special vocation. I simply wanted an excuse for enjoying the pleasures of a London life. The study of the law supplied me with that excuse, and I chose the law as my profession accordingly.

On reaching the place at which we had arranged to meet, I found that my friend had not kept his appointment. After waiting vainly for ten minutes, my patience gave way, and I went into the gardens by myself.

I took two or three turns round the platform devoted to the dancers, without discovering my fellow-student, and without seeing any other person with whom I happened to be acquainted at that time.

For some reason, which I cannot now remember, I was not in my usual good spirits that evening. The noisy music jarred on my nerves; the sight of the gaping crowd round the platform irritated me; the blandishments of the painted ladies of the profession of pleasure saddened and disgusted me. I opened my cigar case, and turned aside into one of the quiet by-walks of the gardens.

A man who is habitually careful in choosing his cigar has this advantage over a man who is habitually careless: he can always count on smoking the best cigar in his case, down to the last. I was still absorbed in choosing *my* cigar, when I heard these words behind me, spoken in a foreign accent, and in a woman's voice :—

"Leave me directly, sir! I wish to have nothing to say to you."

I turned round, and discovered a little lady, very simply and tastefully dressed, who looked both angry and alarmed as she rapidly passed me on her way to the more frequented part of the gardens. A man (evidently the worse for the wine he had drunk in the course of the evening) was following her, and was pressing his tipsy attentions on her with the coarsest insolence of speech and manner. She was young and pretty, and she cast one entreating look at me as she went by, which it was not in manhood—perhaps I ought to say in young manhood —to resist.

I instantly stepped forward to protect her, careless whether I involved myself in a discreditable quarrel with a blackguard or not. As a matter of course, the fellow resented my interference, and my temper gave way. Fortunately for me, just as I lifted my hand to knock him down, a policeman appeared, who had noticed that he was drunk, and who settled the dispute, officially, by turning him out of the gardens.

I led her away from the crowd that had collected. She was evidently frightened—I felt her hand trembling on my arm —but she had one great merit : she made no fuss about it.

"If I can sit down for a few minutes," she said, in her pretty foreign accent, "I shall soon be myself again, and I shall not trespass any further on your kindness. I thank you very much, sir, for taking care of me."

We sat down on a bench in a retired part of the gardens, near a little fountain. A row of lighted lamps ran around the outer rim of the basin. I could see her plainly.

I have spoken of her as "a little lady." I could not have described her more correctly in three words.

Her figure was slight and small. She was a well-made miniature of a woman from head to foot. Her hair and her eyes were both dark. The hair curled naturally; the expression of the eyes was quiet and rather sad; the complexion, as I then saw it, very pale; the little mouth perfectly charming. I was especially attracted, I remember, by the carriage of her head. It was strikingly graceful and spirited. It distinguished her, little as she was, and quiet as she was, among the thousands of other women in the gardens, as a creature apart. Even the one marked defect in her—a slight "cast" in the left eye—seemed to add, in some strange way, to the quaint attractiveness of her face. I have already spoken of the tasteful simplicity of her dress. I ought now to add that it was not made of any costly material, and that she wore no jewels or ornaments of any sort. My little lady was not rich. Even a man's eye could see that.

She was perfectly unembarrassed and unaffected. We fell as easily into talk as if we had been friends instead of strangers.

I asked how it was that she had no companion to take care of her. "You are too young and too pretty," I said in my blunt English way, "to trust yourself alone in such a place as this."

She took no notice of the compliment. She calmly put it away from her as if it had not reached her ears.

"I have no friend to take care of me," she said, simply. "I was sad and sorry this evening, all by myself, and I thought I would go to the gardens and hear the music, just to amuse me. It is not much to pay at the gate. Only a shilling."

"No friend to take care of you?" I repeated. "Surely there must be one happy man who might have been here with you to-night."

"What man do you mean?" she asked.

"The man," I answered, thoughtlessly, "whom we call in England a sweetheart."

I would have given worlds to have recalled those foolish words the moment they passed my lips. I felt that I had taken a vulgar liberty with her. Her face saddened; her eyes dropped to the ground. I begged her pardon.

"There is no need to beg my pardon," she said. "If you wish to know, sir—yes, I had once a sweetheart, as you call it in England. He has gone away and left me. No more of him, if you please. I am rested now. I will thank you again, and go home."

She rose to leave me.

I was determined not to part with her in that way. I begged to be allowed to see her safely back to her own door. She hesitated. I took a man's unfair advantage of her: I appealed to her fears. I said, "Suppose the blackguard who annoyed you should be waiting outside the gates?" That decided her. She took my arm. We went away together by the bank of the Thames in the balmy summer night.

A walk of half an hour brought us to the house in which she lodged—a shabby little house in a by-street, inhabited evidently by very poor people.

She held out her hand at the door, and wished me good-night. I was too much interested in her to consent to leave my little French lady without the hope of seeing her again. I asked permission to call on her the next day. We were standing under the light of the street lamp. She studied my face with a grave and steady attention before she made any reply.

"Yes," she said at last. "I think I do know a gentleman when I see him. You may come, sir, if you please, and call upon me to-morrow."

So we parted. So I entered—doubting nothing, foreboding nothing—on a scene in my life which I now look back on with unfeigned repentance and regret.

III.

I am speaking, at this later time, in the position of a clergy-man, and in the character of a man of mature age. Remember that, and you will understand why I pass as rapidly as possible over the events of the next year of my life; why I say as little as I can of the errors and the delusions of my youth.

I called on her the next day. I repeated my visits during the days and weeks that followed, until the shabby little house in the by-street had become a second and (I say it with shame and self-reproach) a dearer home to me.

All of herself and her story which she thought fit to confide to me under the circumstances, may be repeated to you in a few words.

The name by which letters were addressed to her was "Mademoiselle Jéromette." Among the ignorant people of the house and the small tradesmen of the neighborhood, who found her name not easy of pronunciation by the average English tongue, she was known by the friendly nickname of "the French miss." When I knew her she was resigned to her lonely life among strangers. Some years had elapsed since she had lost her parents and had left France. Possessing a small, a very small, income of her own, she added to it

35

by coloring miniatures for the photographers. She had relatives still living in France, but she had long since ceased to correspond with them. "Ask me nothing more about my family," she used to say. "I am as good as dead in my own country and among my own people."

This was all—literally all—that she told me of herself. I have never discovered more of her sad story from that day to this.

She never mentioned her family name—never even told me what part of France she came from, or how long she had lived in England. That she was by birth and breeding a lady, I could entertain no doubt; her manners, her accomplishments, her ways of thinking and speaking, all proved it. Looking below the surface, her character showed itself in aspects not common among young women in these days. In her quiet way she was an incurable fatalist, and a firm believer in the ghostly reality of apparitions from the dead. Then, again, in the matter of money she had strange views of her own. Whenever my purse was in my hand, she held me resolutely at a distance from first to last. She refused to move into better apartments. The shabby little house was clean inside, and the poor people who lived in it were kind to her, and that was enough. The most expensive present that she ever permitted me to offer her was a little enamelled ring, the plainest and cheapest thing of the kind in the jeweller's shop. In all her relations with me she was sincerity itself. On all occasions, and under all circumstances, she spoke her mind (as the phrase is) with the same uncompromising plainness.

"I like you," she said to me; "I respect you; I shall always be faithful to you while you are faithful to me. But my love has gone from me. There is another man who has taken it away with him, I know not where."

Who was the other man?

She refused to tell me. She kept his rank and his name strict secrets from me. I never discovered how he had met with her, or why he had left her, or whether the guilt was his of making her an exile from her country and her friends. She despised herself for still loving him; but the passion was too strong for her—she owned it and lamented it with the frankness which was so preëminently a part of her character. More than this, she plainly told me, in the early days of our acquaintance, that she believed he would return to her. It might be to-morrow, or it might be years hence. Even if he failed to repent of his own cruel conduct, the man would still miss her as something lost out of his life, and sooner or later he would come back.

" And will you receive him if he does come back?" I asked.

" I shall receive him," she replied, " against my own better judgment—in spite of my own firm persuasion that the day of his return to me will bring with it the darkest days of my life."

I tried to remonstrate with her.

" You have a will of your own," I said. " Exert it if he attempts to return to you."

" I have no will of my own," she answered, quietly, "where *he* is concerned. It is my misfortune to love him." Her eyes rested for a moment on mine with the utter self-abandonment of despair. " We have said enough about this," she added, abruptly ; " let us say no more."

From that time we never spoke again of the unknown man. During the year that followed our first meeting, she heard nothing of him, directly or indirectly. He might be living, or he might be dead. There came no word of him or from him. I was fond enough of her to be satisfied with this—he never disturbed us.

IV.

The year passed, and the end came. Not the end as you may have anticipated it, or as I might have foreboded it.

You remember the time when your letters from home informed you of the fatal termination of our mother's illness? It is the time of which I am now speaking. A few hours only before she breathed her last she called me to her bedside, and desired that we might be left together alone. Reminding me that her death was near, she spoke of my prospects in life; she noticed my want of interest in the studies which were then supposed to be engaging my attention, and she ended by entreating me to reconsider my refusal to enter the Church.

"Your father's heart is set upon it," she said. "Do what I ask of you, my dear, and you will help to comfort him when I am gone."

Her strength failed her; she could say no more. Could I refuse the last request she would ever make to me? I knelt at the bedside and took her wasted hand in mine, and solemnly promised her the respect which a son owes to his mother's last wishes.

Having bound myself by this sacred engagement, I had no choice but to accept the sacrifice which it imperatively exacted from me. The time had come when I must tear myself free from all unworthy associations. No matter what the effort cost me, I must separate myself at once and forever from the unhappy woman who was not, who never could be, my wife.

At the close of a dull, foggy day I set forth, with a heavy heart, to say the words which were to part us forever.

Her lodging was not far from the banks of the Thames. As I drew near the place the darkness was gathering, and the broad surface of the river was hidden from me in a chill, white mist. I stood for a while with my eyes fixed on the vaporous shroud that brooded over the flowing water,—I stood and asked myself, in despair, the one dreary question : "What am I to say to her?"

The mist chilled me to the bones. I turned from the river bank, and made my way to her lodgings hard by. "It must be done," I said to myself, as I took out my key and opened the house door.

She was not at her work as usual, when I entered her little sitting-room. She was standing by the fire, with her head down, and with an open letter in her hand.

The instant she turned to meet me I saw in her face that something was wrong. Her ordinary manner was the manner of an unusually placid and self-restrained person. Her temperament had little of the liveliness which we associate in England with the French nature. She was not ready with her laugh, and in all my previous experience I had never yet known her to cry. Now, for the first time, I saw the quiet face disturbed; I saw tears in the pretty brown eyes. She ran to meet me, and laid her head on my breast, and burst into a passionate fit of weeping that shook her from head to foot.

Could she, by any human possibility, have heard of the coming change in my life? Was she aware, before I had opened my lips, of the hard necessity which had brought me to the house?

It was simply impossible ; the thing could not be.

I waited until her first burst of emotion had worn itself out. Then I asked, with an uneasy conscience, with a sinking heart, what had happened to distress her.

She drew herself away from me, sighing heavily, and gave me the open letter which I had seen in her hand.

"Read that," she said, "and remember I told you what might happen when we first met."

I read the letter.

It was signed in initials only; but the writer plainly re vealed himself as the man who had deserted her. He had repented; he had returned to her. In proof of his penitence he was willing to do her the justice which he had hitherto refused; he was willing to marry her, on the condition that she would engage to keep the marriage a secret so long as his parents lived. Submitting this proposal, he waited to know whether she would consent, on her side, to forgive and forget.

I gave her back the letter in silence. This unknown rival had done me the service of paving the way for our separation. In offering her the atonement of marriage, he had made it, on my part, a matter of duty to *her* as well as to myself to say the parting words. I felt this instantly; and yet I hated him for helping me.

She took my hand and led me to the sofa. We sat down side by side. Her face was composed to a sad tranquillity. She was quiet; she was herself again.

"I have refused to see him," she said, "until I had first spoken to you. You have read his letter. What do you say?"

I could make but one answer. It was my duty to tell her what my own position was in the plainest terms. I did my duty, leaving her free to decide on the future for herself. Those sad words said, it was useless to prolong the wretched-ness of our separation. I rose, and took her hand for the last time.

I see her again now, at that final moment, as plainly as if it had happened yesterday. She had been suffering from an affection of the throat, and she had a white silk handkerchief tied loosely round her neck. She wore a simple dress of

THE CLERGYMAN'S CONFESSION.

purple merino, with a black silk apron over it. Her face was deadly pale; her fingers felt icily cold as they closed round my hand.

"Promise me one thing," I said, "before I go. While I live I am your friend, if I am nothing more. If you are ever in trouble, promise that you will let me know it."

She started, and drew back from me as if I had struck her with a sudden terror.

"Strange!" she said, speaking to herself. "He feels as I feel. He is afraid of what may happen to me in my life to come."

I attempted to re-assure her. I tried to tell her — what was indeed the truth — that I had only been thinking of the ordinary chances and changes of life when I spoke.

She paid no heed to me; she came back and put her hands on my shoulders, and thoughtfully and sadly looked up in my face.

"My mind is not your mind in this matter," she said. "I once owned to you that I had my forebodings when we first spoke of this man's return. I may tell you now more than I told you then. I believe I shall die young, and die miserably. If I am right, have you interest enough still left in me to wish to hear of it?"

She paused, shuddering, and added these startling words: "You *shall* hear of it!"

The tone of steady conviction in which she spoke alarmed and distressed me. My face showed her how deeply and how painfully I was affected.

"There, there!" she said, returning to her natural manner, "don't take what I say too seriously! A poor girl who has led a lonely life like mine thinks strangely and talks strangely sometimes. Yes, I give you my promise. If I am ever in trouble I will let you know it. God bless you—you have been very kind to me. Good-bye!"

A tear dropped on my face as she kissed me. The door closed between us. The dark street received me.

It was raining heavily. I looked up at her window through the drifting shower. The curtains were parted; she was standing in the gap, dimly lit by the lamp on the table behind her, waiting for our last look at each other. Slowly lifting her hand, she waved her farewell at the window with the unsought native grace which had charmed me on the night when we first met. The curtains fell again; she disappeared — nothing was before me, nothing was round me, but the darkness and the night.

V.

In two years from that time I had redeemed the promise given to my mother on her death-bed. I had entered the Church.

My father's interest made my first step in my new profession an easy one. After serving my preliminary apprenticeship as a curate, I was appointed, before I was thirty years of age, to a living in the west of England.

My new benefice offered me every advantage that I could possibly desire, with the one exception of a sufficient income. Although my wants were few, and although I was still an unmarried man, I found it desirable, on many accounts, to add to my resources. Following the example of other young clergymen in my position, I determined to receive pupils who might stand in need of preparation for a career at the Universities. My relatives exerted themselves, and my good fortune still befriended me. I obtained two pupils to start with. A third would complete the number which I was at present prepared to receive. In course of time this third pupil made his appearance, under circumstances sufficiently remarkable to merit being mentioned in detail.

It was the summer vacation, and my two pupils had gone home. Thanks to a neighboring clergyman, who kindly undertook to perform my duties for me, I too obtained a fortnight's holiday, which I spent at my father's house in London.

During my sojourn in the metropolis, I was offered an opportunity of preaching in a church made famous by the eloquence of one of the popular pulpit orators of our time. In accepting the proposal I felt naturally anxious to do my best before the unusually large and unusually intelligent congregation which would be assembled to hear me.

At the period of which I am now speaking, all England had been startled by the discovery of a terrible crime, perpetrated under circumstances of extreme provocation. I chose this crime as the main subject of my sermon. Admitting that the best among us were frail mortal creatures, subject to evil promptings and provocations like the worst among us, my object was to show how a Christian man may find his certain refuge from temptation in the safeguards of his religion. I dwelt minutely on the hardship of the Christian's first struggle to resist the evil influence — on the help which his Christianity inexhaustibly held out to him in the worst relapses of the weaker and viler part of his nature — on the steady and certain gain which was the ultimate reward of his faith and his firmness — and on the blessed sense of peace and happiness which accompanied the final triumph. Preaching to this effect, with the fervent conviction which I really felt, I may say for myself, at least, that I did no discredit to the choice which had placed me in the pulpit. I held the attention of my congregation from the first word to the last.

While I was resting in the vestry, on the conclusion of the

service, a note was brought to me written in pencil. A member of my congregation — a gentleman — wished to see me on a matter of considerable importance to himself. He would call on me at any place, and at any hour, which I might choose to appoint. If I wished to be satisfied of his respectability, he would beg leave to refer me to his father, with whose name I might possibly be acquainted.

The name given in the reference was undoubtedly familiar to me as the name of a man of some celebrity and influence in the world of London. I sent back my card appointing an hour for the visit of my correspondent on the afternoon of the next day.

44

PART SECOND.

VI.

THE stranger made his appearance punctually. I guessed him to be some two or three years younger than myself. He was undeniably handsome; his manners were the manners of a gentleman; and yet, without knowing why, I felt a strong dislike to him the moment he entered the room.

After the first preliminary words of politeness had been exchanged between us, my visitor informed me as follows of the object which he had in view : —

"I believe you live in the country, sir?" he began.

"I live in the west of England," I answered.

"Do you make a long stay in London?"

"No. I go back to my rectory to-morrow."

"May I ask if you take pupils?"

"Yes."

"Have you any vacancy?"

"I have one vacancy."

"Would you object to let me go back with you to-morrow as your pupil?"

The abruptness of the proposal took me by surprise. I hesitated.

In the first place (as I have already said), I disliked him. In the second place, he was too old to be a fit companion for my other two pupils — both lads in their teens. In the third place, he had asked me to receive him at least three weeks before the vacation came to an end. I had my own pursuits and amusements in prospect during that interval, and saw no reason why I should inconvenience myself by setting them aside.

He noticed my hesitation, and did not conceal from me that I had disappointed him.

"I have it very much at heart," he said, "to repair without delay the time that I have lost. My age is against me, I know. The truth is, I have wasted my opportunities since I left school, and I am anxious, honestly anxious, to mend my ways before it is too late. I wish to prepare myself for one of the Universities; I wish to show, if I can, that I am not quite unworthy to inherit my father's famous name. You are the man to help me, if I can only persuade you to do it. I was struck by your sermon yesterday, and, if I may venture to make the confession in your presence, I took a strong liking to you. Will you see my father before you decide to say no? He will be able to explain whatever may seem strange in my present application, and he will be happy to see you this afternoon, if you can spare the time. As to the question of terms, I am quite sure it can be settled to your entire satisfaction."

He was evidently in earnest — gravely, vehemently in earnest. I unwillingly consented to see his father.

The interview was a long one. All my questions were answered fully and frankly.

The young man had led an idle and desultory life. He was weary of it, and ashamed of it. His disposition was a peculiar one. He stood sorely in need of a guide, a teacher and a friend in whom he was disposed to confide. If I disappointed the hopes which he had centred in me he would be discouraged, and he would relapse into the aimless and indolent existence of which he was now ashamed. Any terms for which I might stipulate were at my disposal, if I would consent to receive him for three months, to begin with, on trial.

I still hesitated. I consulted my father and my friends.

They were all of opinion (and justly of opinion so far) that

46

the new connection would be an excellent one for me. They
all reproached me for taking a purely capricious dislike to a
well-born and well-bred young man, and for permitting it to
influence me at the outset of my career against my own inter-
ests. Pressed by these considerations, I allowed myself to be
persuaded to give the new pupil a fair trial. He accompanied
me the next day on my way back to the rectory.

VII.

My senior pupil (you will find out his name for yourself
before I have done) began well in one respect, at least — he
produced a decidedly favorable impression on the persons
attached to my little household.

The women especially admired his beautiful light hair, his
crisply curling beard, his delicate complexion, his clear blue
eyes, and his finely shaped hands and feet. Even the inveterate reserve in his manner, and the downcast, almost sullen,
look which had prejudiced *me* against him, aroused a common feeling of romantic enthusiasm in my servants' hall. It
was decided on the high authority of the housekeeper herself
that "the new gentleman" was in love, and, more interesting
still, that he was the victim of an unhappy attachment which
had driven him away from his friends and his home.

For myself, I tried hard, and tried vainly, to get over my
first dislike to the senior pupil.

I could find no fault with him. All his habits were quiet
and regular, and he devoted himself conscientiously to his
reading. But, little by little, I became satisfied that his heart
was not in his studies. More than this, I had my reasons for
suspecting that he was concealing something from me, and
that he felt painfully the reserve on his own part, which he
could not, or dared not, break through. There were moments

when I almost doubted whether he had not chosen my remote country rectory as a safe place of refuge from some person or persons of whom he stood in dread.

For example, his ordinary course of proceeding in the matter of his correspondence was, to say the least of it, strange.

He received no letters at my house. They waited for him at the village post-office. He invariably called for them himself, and invariably forbore to trust any of my servants with his own letters for the post. Again, when we were out walking together, I more than once caught him looking furtively over his shoulder, as if he suspected some person of following him for some evil purpose. Being constitutionally a hater of mysteries, I determined at an early stage of our intercourse on making an effort to clear matters up. There might be just a chance of my winning the senior pupil's confidence, if I spoke to him while the last days of the summer vacation still left us alone together in the house.

"Excuse me for noticing it," I said to him one morning, while we were engaged over our books, "I cannot help observing that you appear to have some trouble on your mind. Is it indiscreet on my part to ask if I can be of any use to you?"

He changed color, looked up at me quickly, looked down again at his book, struggled hard with some secret fear or secret reluctance that was in him, and suddenly burst out with this extraordinary question : —

"I suppose you were in earnest when you preached that sermon in London?"

"I am astonished that you should doubt it," I replied.

He paused again, struggled with himself again, and startled me by a second outbreak, even stranger than the first.

" I am one of the people you preached at in your sermon," he said. "That's the true reason why I asked you to take me for your pupil. Don't turn me out! When you talked to your congregation of tortured and tempted people, you talked of me."

I was so astonished by the confession that I lost my presence of mind. For the moment I was unable to answer him.

"Don't turn me out!" he repeated. "Help me against myself. I am telling you the truth. As God is my witness, I am telling you the truth!"

"Tell me the *whole* truth," I said, "and rely on my consoling and helping you — rely on my being your friend."

In the fervor of the moment I took his hand. It lay cold and still in mine; it mutely warned me that I had a sullen and secret nature to deal with.

"There must be no concealment between us," I resumed. "You have entered my house, by your own confession, under false pretences. It is your duty to me, and your duty to yourself, to speak out."

The man's inveterate reserve, cast off for the moment only, renewed its hold on him. He considered, carefully considered, his next words before he permitted them to pass his lips.

"A person is in the way of my prospects in life," he began, slowly, with his eyes cast down on his book. "A person provokes me horribly. I feel dreadful temptations (like the man you spoke of in your sermon) when I am in the person's company. Teach me to resist temptation! I am afraid of myself if I see the person again. You are the only man who can help me. Do it while you can."

He stopped, and passed his handkerchief over his forehead.

"Will that do?" he asked, still with his eyes on his book.

"It will *not* do," I answered. "You are so far from really opening your heart to me that you won't even let me know whether it is a man or a woman who stands in the way of

49

your prospects in life. You use the word 'person' over and over again, rather than say 'he' or 'she,' when you speak of the provocation which is trying you. How can I help a man who has so little confidence in me as that?"

He twisted and untwisted his handkerchief in his hands. He tried, tried desperately, to say more than he had said yet. No! The words seemed to stick in his throat. Not one of them would pass his lips.

"Give me time," he pleaded, piteously. "I can't bring myself to it all at once. I mean well. Upon my soul, I mean well. But I am slow at this sort of thing. Wait till to-morrow."

To-morrow came, and again he put it off.

"One more day," he said. "You don't know how hard it is to speak plainly. I am half afraid; I am half ashamed. Give me one more day."

I had hitherto only disliked him. Try as I might, and did, to make merciful allowance for his reserve, I began to despise him now.

VIII.

The day of the deferred confession came, and brought an event with it for which both he and I were alike unprepared. Would he really have confided in me but for that event? He must either have done it, or have abandoned the purpose which had led him into my house.

We met as usual at the breakfast table. My housekeeper brought in my letters of the morning. To my surprise, instead of leaving the room again as usual, she walked around to the other side of the table, and laid a letter before my senior pupil—the first letter since his residence with me which had been delivered to him under my roof.

He started, and took up the letter. He looked at the address. A spasm of suppressed fury passed across his face; his breath came quickly; his hand trembled as it held the letter. So far I said nothing. I waited to see whether he would open the envelope in my presence or not.

He was afraid to open it in my presence. He got on his feet; he said, in tones so low that I could barely hear him, "Please excuse me for a minute," and left the room.

I waited for half an hour—for a quarter of an hour after that—and then I sent to ask if he had forgotten his breakfast.

In a minute more I heard his footstep in the hall. He opened the breakfast-room door, and stood on the threshold, with a small travelling-bag in his hand.

"I beg your pardon," he said, still standing at the door. "I must ask for leave of absence for a day or two. Business in London."

"Can I be of any use?" I asked. "I am afraid your letter has brought you bad news."

"Yes," he said, shortly; "bad news. I have no time for breakfast."

"Wait a few minutes," I urged. "Wait long enough to treat me like your friend, to tell me what your trouble is, before you go."

He made no reply. He stepped into the hall and closed the door; then opened it again a little way without showing himself.

"Business in London," he repeated, as if he thought it highly important to inform me of the nature of his errand. The door closed for the second time. He was gone.

I went into my study and carefully considered what had happened.

The result of my reflections is easily described. I determined on discontinuing my relations with my senior pupil.

In writing to his father (which I did, with all due courtesy and respect, by that day's post), I mentioned as my reason for arriving at this decision, first, that I had found it impossible to win the confidence of his son. Secondly, that his son had that morning suddenly and mysteriously left my house for London, and that I must decline accepting any further responsibility toward him, as the necessary consequence.

I had put my letter in the post-bag, and I was beginning to feel a little easier after having written it, when my housekeeper appeared in the study, with a very grave face, and with something hidden, apparently, in her closed hand.

"Would you please look, sir, at what we have found in the gentleman's bedroom since he went away this morning?"

I knew the housekeeper to possess a woman's full share of that amiable weakness of the sex which goes by the name of "curiosity." I had also, in various indirect ways, become aware that my senior pupil's strange departure had largely increased the disposition among the women of my household to regard him as the victim of an unhappy attachment. The time was ripe, as it seemed to me, for checking any further gossip about him, and any renewed attempts at prying into his affairs in his absence.

"Your only business in my pupil's bedroom," I said to the housekeeper, "is to see that it is kept clean, and that it is properly aired. There must be no interference, if you please, with his letters or his papers, or with anything else that he has left behind him. Put back directly whatever you may have found in his room."

The housekeeper had her full share of a woman's temper, as well as of a woman's curiosity. She listened to me with a rising color, and a just perceptible toss of the head.

"Must I put it back, sir, on the floor, between the bed and the wall?" she inquired, with an ironical assumption of the

52

humblest deference to my wishes. "*That's* where the girl found it when she was sweeping the room. Anybody can see for themselves," pursued the housekeeper, indignantly, "that the poor gentleman has gone away broken-hearted. And there, in my opinion, is the hussy who is the cause of it!"

With those words she made me a low courtesy, and laid a small photographic portrait on the desk at which I was sitting.

I looked at the photograph.

In an instant my heart was beating wildly—my head turned giddy—the housekeeper, the furniture, the walls of the room, all swayed and whirled round me.

The portrait that had been found in my senior pupil's bed-room was the portrait of Jéromette!

IX.

I had sent the housekeeper out of my study. I was alone, with the photograph of the Frenchwoman on my desk.

There could surely be little doubt about the discovery that had burst upon me. The man who had stolen his way into my house, driven by the terror of a temptation that he dared not reveal, and the man who had been my unknown rival in the by-gone time, were one and the same.

Recovering self-possession enough to realize this plain truth, the inferences that followed forced their way into my mind as a matter of course. The unnamed person who was the obstacle to my pupil's prospects in life, the unnamed person in whose company he was assailed by temptations which made him tremble for himself, stood revealed to me now as being, in all human probability, no other than Jéromette. Had she bound him in the fetters of the marriage which he had himself proposed? Had she discovered his place of refuge in

53

my house? And was the letter that had been delivered to him of her writing? Assuming those questions to be answered in the affirmative, what, in that case, was his "business in London"? I remembered what he had said to me about his temptations, I recalled the expression that had crossed his face when he recognized the handwriting on the letter — and the conclusion that followed literally shook me to the soul. Ordering my horse to be saddled, I rode instantly to the railway station.

The train by which he had travelled to London had reached the terminus nearly an hour since. The one useful course that I could take, by way of quieting the dreadful misgivings crowding one after another on my mind, was to telegraph to Jéromette at the address at which I had last seen her. I sent the subjoined message, prepaying the reply :—

"If you are in any trouble, telegraph to me. I will be with you by the first train. Answer, in any case."

There was nothing in the way of the immediate dispatch of my message. And yet the hours passed, and no answer was received. By the advice of the clerk, I sent a second telegram to the London office, requesting an explanation. The reply came back in these terms :—

"Improvements in street. Houses pulled down. No trace of person named in telegram."

I mounted my horse and rode back slowly to the rectory.

"The day of his return to me will bring with it the darkest days of my life."—"I shall die young, and die miserably. — "Have you interest enough still left in me to wish to hear of it?"—"You *shall* hear of it!" Those words were in my memory while I rode home in the cloudless moonlight night. They were so vividly present to me that I could hear again her pretty foreign accent, her quiet, clear tones, as she spoke them. For the rest, the emotions of that memorable day had worn me out. The answer from the telegraph office had struck me with a strange and stony despair. My mind was a blank. I had no thoughts. I had no tears.

I was about half-way on my road home, and I had just heard the clock of a village church strike ten, when I became conscious, little by little, of a chilly sensation slowly creeping through and through me to the bones. The warm balmy air of a summer night was abroad. It was the month of July. In the month of July was it possible that any living creature, in good health, could feel cold? It was *not* possible — and yet the chilly sensation still crept through and through me to the bones.

I looked up. I looked all around me.

My horse was walking along an open high-road. Neither trees nor waters were near me. On either side the flat fields stretched away bright and broad in the moonlight.

I stopped my horse, and looked around me again.

Yes, I saw it. With my own eyes I saw it. A pillar of white mist — between five and six feet high, as well as I could judge — was moving beside me at the edge of the road, on my left hand. When I stopped, the white mist stopped. When I went on, the white mist went on. I pushed my horse to a trot, the pillar of mist was with me. I urged him to a gallop, the pillar of mist was with me. I stopped him again, the pillar of mist stood still.

The white color of it was the white color of the mist which I had seen over the river on the night when I had gone to bid her farewell. And the chill which had then crept through me to the bones was the chill that was creeping through me now.

I went on again slowly. The white mist went on again slowly, with the clear bright night all round it.

I was awed rather than frightened. There was one moment, and one only, when the fear came to me that my reason might be shaken. I caught myself keeping time to the slow tramp of the horse's feet with the slow utterance of these words, repeated over and over again: "Jéromette is dead. Jéromette is dead." But my will was still my own; I was able to control myself, to impose silence on my own muttering lips. And I rode on quietly. And the pillar of mist went quietly with me.

My groom was waiting for my return at the rectory gate. I pointed to the mist, passing through the gate with me.

"Do you see anything there?" I said.

The man looked at me in astonishment.

I entered the rectory. The housekeeper met me in the hall. I pointed to the mist entering with me.

"Do you see anything at my side?" I asked.

The housekeeper looked at me as the groom had looked at me. "I am afraid you are not well, sir," she said. "Your color is all gone; you are shivering. Let me get you a glass of wine."

I went into my study, on the ground-floor, and took the chair at my desk. The photograph still lay where I had left it. The pillar of mist floated round the table, and stopped opposite to me, behind the photograph.

The housekeeper brought in the wine. I put the glass to my lips, and set it down again. The chill of the mist was in the wine. There was no taste, no reviving spirit in it. The presence of the housekeeper oppressed me. My dog had followed her into the room. The presence of the animal oppressed me. I said to the woman, "Leave me by myself, and take the dog with you."

They went out, and left me alone in the room.

I sat looking at the pillar of mist hovering opposite to me.
It lengthened slowly until it reached to the ceiling. As it
lengthened it grew bright and luminous. A time passed, and
a shadowy appearance showed itself in the centre of the light.
Little by little the shadowy appearance took the outline of a
human form. Soft brown eyes, tender and melancholy,
looked at me through the unearthly light in the mist. The
head and the rest of the face broke next slowly on my view.
Then the figure gradually revealed itself, moment by moment, downward and downward to the feet. She stood before
me as I had last seen her, in her purple merino dress, with
the black silk apron, with the white handkerchief tied loosely
round her neck. She stood before me in the gentle beauty
that I remembered so well, and looked at me as she had
looked when she gave me her last kiss, when her tears had
dropped on my cheek.

I fell on my knees at the table. I stretched out my hands
to her imploringly. I said, "Speak to me, oh, once again
speak to me, Jéromette!"

Her eyes rested on me with a divine compassion in them.
She lifted her hand, and pointed to the photograph on my
desk with a gesture which bade me turn the card. I turned
it. The name of the man who had left my house that morning was inscribed on it in her own handwriting.

I looked up at her again when I had read it. She lifted
her hand once more, and pointed to the handkerchief round
her neck. As I looked at it the fair white silk changed horribly in color; the fair white silk became darkened and
drenched in blood.

A moment more, and the vision of her began to grow dim.
By slow degrees the figure, then the face, faded back into the
shadowy appearance that I had first seen. The luminous

inner light died out in the white mist. The mist itself dropped slowly downward, floated a moment in airy circles on the floor, vanished. Nothing was before me but the familiar wall of the room, and the photograph lying face downward on my desk.

X.

The next day the newspapers reported the discovery of a murder in London. A Frenchwoman was the victim. She had been killed by a wound in the throat. The crime had been discovered between ten and eleven o'clock on the previous night.

I leave you to draw your conclusion from what I have related. My own faith in the reality of the apparition is immovable. I say and believe that Jéromette kept her word with me. She died young, and died miserably. And I heard of it from herself.

Take up the trial again, and look at the circumstances that were revealed during the investigation in court. His motive for murdering her is there.

You will see that she did indeed marry him privately; that they lived together contentedly until the fatal day when she discovered that his fancy had been caught by another woman; that violent quarrels took place between them from that time to the time when my sermon showed him his own deadly hatred toward her, reflected in the case of another man; that she discovered his place of retreat in my house, and threatened him by letter with the public assertion of her conjugal rights; lastly, that a man, variously described by different witnesses, was seen leaving the door of her lodgings on the night of the murder. The law, advancing no further than this, may have discovered circumstances of suspicion, but no certainty. The law, in default of direct evidence to convict the prisoner, may have rightly decided in letting him go free.

But *I* persist in believing that the man was guilty. *I* declare that he, and he alone, was the murderer of Jéromette. And now you know why.

POEM.

POEM.

SUNG AT THE DEDICATION OF THE HAVERHILL (MASS.) LIBRARY, NOV. 11, 1875.

BY JOHN G. WHITTIER.

"ET there be light!" God spake of old,
And over Chaos dark and cold,
And through the dead and formless frame
Of Nature, life and order came.

Faint was the light at first that shone
On giant fern and mastodon,
On half-formed plant and beast of prey,
And man as rude and wild as they.

Age after age, like waves, o'erran
The earth, uplifting brute and man;
And mind, at length, in symbols dark,
Its meanings traced on stone and bark.

On leaf of palm, on sedge-wrought roll.
On plastic clay and leathern scroll,
Man wrote his thought: the ages passed,
And lo! the Press was found at last.

Then dead souls woke; the thoughts of men
Whose bones were dust, revived again:
The cloister's silence found a tongue,
Old prophets spake, old poets sung.

And here, to-day, the dead look down,
And kings of mind again we crown;
We hear the sage's word; we trace
The footprints of our human race.

Here Greek and Roman find themselves
Alive along these crowded shelves;
And Shakspeare treads again his stage,
And Chaucer paints anew his age.

63

POEM.

As if some Pantheon's marbles broke
Their stony trance, and lived and spoke,
Life thrills around the alcoved hall,
The lords of thought awake our call!

SUBMISSION.

SUBMISSION.

BY KATE TANNATT WOODS.

HEN through the fields I wend my way,
In the bright hours of growing day,
My hand fast holding one who knows
With me no fear of harm or foes, —
Nature, kind mother! brings to me
A sense of rest, and I am free.

Each budding flower then bids me wait,
My richest gifts may reach me late,
And still be rich; each bud, though small,
Sends fragrance on the air for all.
And if my heart be sad and sore,
I wait and hope, nor ask for more.

Above my head the swallows fly,
Far higher in God's world than I;
Yet one stray shot may break a wing,
And cast to earth, a helpless thing:
Just as some heart receives a blow,
Which leaves it numb and full of woe.

Beneath my feet the cooling grass
Bends meekly where I choose to pass;
And at my side the violets grow,
Forgetting they were nursed by snow:
In patience they have learned to wait,
Trusting their Maker with their fate.

My little child, with eager feet,
Urges me on, his pets to greet;
And in their eyes I still can see
The lesson of the day for me:
Whate'er God wills, come soon, come late,
'Tis only mine to work and wait.

SUBMISSION.

This lesson learned, the humblest flower
Shows some new beauty every hour;
This learned, throughout the darkest night,
I wait in silence for the light,
Endure all toil, griefs, small and great:
Heaven's door stands wide for those who wait.

PRISCILLA.

PRISCILLA.

BY EDMUND EGGLESTON.

HE trained novel readers, those who have made a business of it (if any such should honor this poor little story with their attention), will glance down the opening paragraphs for a description of the heroine's tresses. The opening sentences of Miss Braddon are enough to show how important a thing a head of hair is in the getting up of a heroine for the popular market. But as my heroine is not gotten up for the market, and as I cannot possibly remember even the color of her hair or her eyes as I recall her now, I fear I shall disappoint the "professionals," who never feel that they have a complete heroine till the "long waving tresses of raven darkness, reaching nearly to the ground, enveloping her as with a cloud," have been artistically stuck on by the author. But be it known that I take Priscilla from memory, and not from imagination. And the memory of Priscilla, the best girl in the school, the most gifted, the most modest, the most gentle and true, is a memory too sacred to be trifled with. I would not make one hair light or dark ; I would not change the shading of the eye-brows. Priscilla is Priscilla forever, to all who knew her. And as I cannot tell the precise color of her hair and eyes, I shall not invent a shade for them. I remember that she was on the blonde side of the grand division line. But she was not blonde. She was—Priscilla. I mean to say that since you

never lived in that dear old-fogy Ohio River village of New
Geneva, and since, consequently, you never knew our Priscilla, no words of mine can make you exactly understand
her. Was she handsome? No—yes; She was "jimber-
jawed ;" that is, her lower teeth shut a little outside her upper.
Her complexion was not faultless. Her face would not bear
criticism. And yet there is not one of her old schoolmates
that will not vow that she was beautiful. And indeed she
was. For she was Priscilla. And I never can make you understand it.

As Priscilla was always willing to oblige any one, it was
only natural enough that Mrs. Leston should send for her to
help entertain the Marquis. It was a curious chance that
threw the young Marquis d'Entremont for a whole summer
into the society of our little village. His uncle, who was his
guardian, a pious *abbé*, wishing to remove him from Paris to
get him out of socialistic influences, had sent him to New Orleans, consigned to the care of the great banking-house of
Challeau, Lafort et Compagnie. Not liking to take the
chances of yellow fever in the summer, he had resolved to
journey to the north, and as Challeau, Lafort et Cie. had a
correspondent in Henry Leston, the young lawyer, and as
French was abundantly spoken in our Swiss village of New
Geneva, what more natural than that they should despatch the
Marquis to our pleasant town of vineyards, giving him a
letter of introduction to their attorney, who fortunately spoke
some book French? He had presented the letter, had been
invited to dinner, and Priscilla Haines, who had learned
French in childhood, though she was not Swiss, was sent for
to help entertain the guest.

I cannot but fancy that d'Entremont was surprised at meeting just such a girl as Priscilla in a rustic village. She was
not abashed at finding herself *vis-à-vis* with a nobleman, nor

did she seem at all anxious to attract his notice. The vanity
of the Marquis must have been a little hurt at finding a lady
that did not court his attention. But wounded vanity soon
gave place to another surprise. Even Mrs. Leston, who understood not one word of the conversation between her husband, the Marquis and Priscilla, was watching for this second
surprise, and did not fail to read it in d'Entremont's eyes.
Here was a young woman who had read. She could admire
Corinne, she could oppose Saint Simon. The Marquis
d'Entremont had resigned himself to the *ennui* of talking to
Swiss farmers about their vineyards, of listening to Swiss grand-
mothers telling stories of their childhood in Neufchatel and
Berne. But to find in this young village school teacher one
who could speak, and listen while he spoke, of his favorite
writers, was to him very strange. Not that Priscilla had
read many French books, for there were not many within her
reach. But she had read some, and she had read Ste. Beuve
and Grimm's Correspondence, and he who reads these two
has heard the echo of all the great voices in French literature.
And while David Haines had lived, his daughter had wanted
nothing to help her to the highest culture.

But I think what amazed the Marquis most was that Priscilla showed no consciousness of the unusual character of her
attainments. She spoke easily and naturally of what she
knew, as if it were a matter of course that the teacher of a
primary school should have read Corneille, and should be
able to combat Saint-Simonism. As the dinner drew to a
close, Leston lifted his chair round where his wife sat, and
interpreted the brilliant conversation at the other side of the
table.

I suspect that Saint Simon had lost some of his hold upon
the Marquis since his arrival in a country where life is more
beautiful and the manner of thought more practical. At any

rate, he dated the decline of his socialistic opinions from his discussion with Priscilla Haines.

The next Sunday morning he strolled out of the Le Vert house, breathing the sweet air perfumed with the blossoms of a thousand apple-trees. For what yard is there in New Geneva that has not apple trees and grape-vines? And every family in the village keeps a cow, and every cow wears a bell, and every bell is on a different key; so that the three things that penetrated the senses of the Marquis on this Sunday morning were the high hills that stood sentinels on every hand about the valley in which New Geneva stood, the smell of the apple blossoms, and the *tinkle* and *tankle* and *tonkle* of hundreds of bells on the cows grazing on the "commons," as the open lots were called. On this almost painfully quiet morning, d'Entremont noticed the people going one way and another to the Sunday schools in the three churches. Just as he came to the pump that stood in front of the "public square," he met Priscilla. At her heels were ten ragged little ruffians, whom she was accustomed to have come to her house every Sunday morning and walk with her to Sunday school.

"You are then a Sister of Charity also?" he said in French, bowing low with sincere admiration as he passed her. And then to himself the young Marquis reflected: "We Saint-Simonists theorize and build castles in Spain for poor people, but we do not take hold of them." He walked clear round the square, and then followed the steps of Priscilla into the little brick Methodist church, which in that day had neither steeple nor bell, which had nothing church-like about it except the two arched front windows. There was not even a fence to enclose it, nor an evergreen nor an ivy about it; only a few black locusts. For the Congregational puritanism of New England was never so hard a puritanism as the Methodist puritanism of a generation ago in the West — a

74

puritanism that forbade jewelry, that stripped the artificial
flowers out of the bonnets of country girls, that expelled and
even yet expels a country boy for looking with wonder at a
man hanging head downward from a trapeze in a circus tent.
No other church, not even the Quaker, ever laid its hand
more entirely upon the whole life of its members. The dead
hand of Wesley has been stronger than the living hand of
any pope.

Upon the hard, open-backed, unpainted and unvarnished
oak benches, which seemed devised to produce discomfort,
sat the Sunday-school classes, and upon one of these, near
the door, d'Entremont sat down. He looked at the bare
walls, at the white pulpit, at the carpetless floors, at the
general ugliness of things, the box-stove, which stood in the
only aisle, the tin chandeliers with their half-burned candles,
the eight-by-ten lights of glass in the windows, and he was
favorably impressed. With a quick conscience he had often
felt the frivolous emptiness of a worldly life, and had turned
toward the religion of his uncle the *abbé* only to turn away
again disgusted with the frivolity of the religious pomp that
he saw. But here was a religion not only without the attractions of sensuous surrounding, but a religion that maintained
its vitality despite a repelling plainness, not to say a repulsive
ugliness, in its external forms. For could he doubt the force
of a religious principle that had divested every woman in the
little church of every ornament? Doubtless he felt the nar-
rowness that could read the Scriptural injunction so literally,
but none could doubt the strength of a religious principle that
submitted to such self-denial. And then there was Priscilla,
with all her gifts, sitting in the midst of her boys, gathered
from that part of the village known as "Slabtown." Yes,
there must be something genuine in this religious life, and its

entire contrast to all that the Marquis had known and grown weary of, attracted him.

As eleven o'clock drew on, the little church filled with people. The men sat on one side the aisle and the women on the other. The old brethren and sisters, and generally those who prayed in prayer meeting and spoke in love-feast, sat near the front, many of them on the cross-seats near the pulpit, which were thence said by scoffers to be the "Amen corners." Any one other than a leader of the hosts of Israel would as soon have thought of taking a seat in the pulpit as on one of these chief seats in the synagogue. The Marquis sat still and watched the audience gather, while one of the good brethren led the congregation in singing,

"When I can read my title clear,"

which hymn was the usual voluntary at the opening of service. Then the old minister said, "Let us continue the worship of God by singing hymn on page 554." He "lined" the hymn, that is, he read each couplet before it was sung. With the coming in of hymn-books and other new-fangled things the good old custom of "lining the hymn" has disappeared. But on that Sunday morning the Marquis d'Entremont thought he had never heard anything more delightful than these simple melodies sung thus lustily by earnest voices. The reading of each couplet by the minister before it was sung, seemed to him a sort of recitative. He knew enough of English to find that the singing was hopeful and triumphant. Wearied with philosophy and *blasé* with the pomp of the world, he wished that he had been a villager in New Geneva, and that he might have had the faith to sing of the

" — land of pure delight
Where saints immortal reign,"

with as much earnestness as his friend Priscilla on the other side of the aisle. In the prayer that followed, d'Entremont noticed that all the church members knelt, and that the hearty *amens* were not intoned, but were as spontaneous as the rest of the service. After reverently reading a chapter the old minister said, " Please sing, without lining,

" ' A charge to keep I have ; ' "

and then the old tune of "Kentucky" was sung with anima-tion, after which came the sermon, of which the Marquis un-derstood but few words, though he understood the pantomine by which the venerable minister represented the return of the prodigal and the welcome he received. When he saw the tears in the eyes of the hearers, and heard the half-repressed "Bless the Lord" of an old brother or sister, and saw them glance joyfully at each others' faces as the sermon went on, he was strangely impressed with the genuineness of the feel-ing.

But the class meeting that followed, to which he remained, impressed him still more. The venerable Scotchman who led it had a face that beamed with sweetness and intelligence. It was fortunate that the Marquis saw so good a specimen. In fact, Priscilla trembled lest Mr. Boreas, the stern, hard-featured "exhorter," should have been invited to lead. But as the sweet-faced old leader called upon one and another to speak, and as many spoke with streaming eyes, d'Entremont quivered with sympathy. He was not so blind that he could not see the sham and cant of some of the speeches, but in general there was much earnestness and truth. When Pris-cilla rose in her turn and spoke, with downcast eyes, he felt the beauty and simplicity of her religious life. And he rightly judged that from the soil of a *culte* so severe, there must grow some noble and heroic lives.

Last of all the class leader reached the Marquis, whom he did not know.

"Will our strange brother tell us how it is with him to-day?" he asked.

Priscilla trembled. What awful thing might happen when a class-leader invited a marquis, who could speak no English, and who was a disciple of Saint Simon, to tell his religious experience, was more than she could divine. If the world had come to an end in consequence of such a concatenation, I think she would not have been surprised. But nothing of the sort occurred. To her astonishment the Marquis rose and said : —

"Is it that any one can speak French?"

A brother who was a member of one of the old Swiss families volunteered his services as interpreter, and d'Entremont proceeded to tell them how much he had been interested in the exercises; that it was the first time he had ever been in such a meeting, and that he wished he had the simple faith which they showed.

Then the old leader said, "Let us engage in prayer for our strange brother."

And the Marquis bowed his knees upon the hard floor.

He could not understand much that was said, but he knew that they were praying for him; that this white-haired class-leader, and the old ladies in the corner, and Priscilla, were interceding with the Father of all for him. He felt more confidence in the efficacy of their prayers than he had ever had in all the intercessions of the saints of which he was told when a boy. For surely God would hear such as Priscilla!

It happened not long after this that d'Entremont was drawn even more nearly to this simple Methodist life, which had already made such an impression on his imagination, by an incident which would make a chapter if this story were intended for the "New York Weekly Dexter." Indeed, the story of his peril in a storm and freshet on Indian Creek, and of his deliverance by the courage of Henry Stevens, is so well suited to that periodical and others of its class, that I am almost sorry that Mrs. Eden, or Cobb, Jr., or Optic, was not the author of this story. Either of them could make a chapter which would bear the title of "A Thrilling Incident." But with an unconquerable aversion to anything and every-thing "thrilling," this present writer can only say in plainest prose and without a single startling epithet, that this incident made the young Marquis the everlasting friend of his deliv-erer, Henry Stevens, who happened to be a zealous Metho-dist, and about his own age.

The effort of the two friends to hold intercourse was a curi-ous spectacle. Not only did they speak different languages, but they lived in different worlds. Not only did d'Entremont speak a very limited English while Stevens spoke no French, but d'Entremont's life and thought had nothing in common with the life of Stevens, except the one thing that made a friendship possible. They were both generous, manly men, and each felt a strong drawing to the other. So it came about that when they tired of the Marquis' English, and of the gulf between their ideas, they used to call on Priscilla at her home with her mother in the outskirts of the village. She was an interpreter indeed! For with the keenest sympa-thy she entered into the world in which the Marquis lived, which had always been a sort of intellectual paradise to her. It seemed strange, indeed, to meet a living denizen of a world that seemed to her impossible except in books. And as for the sphere in which Stevens moved, it was her own. He and she had been schoolmates from childhood, had looked on the same green hills, known the same people, been moulded of the same strong religious feeling. Nothing was more delight-

ful to d'Entremont than to be able to talk to Stevens, unless it
was to have so good an excuse for conversation with Priscilla;
and nothing was so pleasant to Henry Stevens as to be able
to understand the Marquis, unless it was to talk with Priscilla;
while to Priscilla those were golden moments, in which she
passed like a quick-winged messenger between her own native world and the world that she knew only in books, between the soul of one friend and that of another. And thus
grew up a triple friendship, a friendship afterward sorely
tried. For how strange it is that what brings together at one
time may be a wall of division at another.

I am not writing an essay on Christian experience. I cannot pretend to explain just how it came about. Doubtless
Henry Stevens' influence had something to do with it, though
I feel sure Priscilla's had more. Doubtless the Marquis was
naturally susceptible to religious influences, and I cannot but
feel that after all he was led by the gentle drawings of the
Divine Oracle in his own breast. But the erratic opinions,
never very deeply rooted, and at most but a reaction from a
religion of "postures and impostures," disappeared, and there
came a sense of unworthiness and a sense of trust. They
came simultaneously, I think; certainly d'Entremont could
never give any chronological order to the two experiences.
At any rate, he was drawn to the little class meeting, which
seemed to him so simple a confessional that all his former
notions of "liberty, fraternity and equality" were satisfied by
it. I believe he became a "probationer," but his creed was
never quite settled enough for him to accept of "full member-
ship."

Some of the old folks could not refrain from expressions of
triumph that "the Lord had got a-hold of that French infi-
del;" and old Sister Goodenough seized his hand, and, with
many sighs and much upturning of the eyes, exhorted him:

"Brother Markus! Give up everything! Give up everything, and come out from the world and be separated!" Which led d'Entremont to remark to Stevens as they walked away, that "Madame Goodenough was vare curus indeed!" And Brother Boreas, the exhorter, who had the misfortune not to have a business reputation without blemish, but who made up for it by rigid scruples in regard to a melodeon in the church, and by a vicarious conscience which was kindly kept at everybody's service but his own, old Brother Boreas always remarked in regard to the Marquis, that "as for his part he liked a deeper repentance and a sounder conversion." But the gray-haired old Scotch class leader, whose piety was at a premium everywhere, would take d'Entremont's hand and talk of indifferent subjects while he *beamed* on him his affection and Christian fellowship.

To the Marquis, Priscilla was a perpetual marvel. More brilliant women he had known in Paris, more devout women he had seen there; but a woman so gifted and so devout, and above all, a woman so true, so modest, and of such perfect delicacy of feeling, he had never known. And how poorly these words describe her! For she was Priscilla; and all who knew her will understand how much more that means than any adjectives of mine. Certainly Henry Stevens did, for he had known her always, and would have loved her always had he dared. It was only now, as she interpreted him to the Marquis and the Marquis to him, idealizing and elevating the thoughts of both, that he surrendered himself to hope. And so, toward the close of the summer, affairs came to this awkward posture, that these two sworn friends loved the same woman.

D'Entremont discovered this first. More a man of the world than Henry Stevens, he read the other's face and voice. He was perturbed. Had it occurred two years before, he might have settled the matter easily, by a duel for instance. And even now his passion got the better for a while of all his good feelings and Christian resolutions. When he got back to the Le Vert house with his unpleasant discovery, he was burning like a furnace. In spite of a rain-storm just beginning and a dark night, he strode out and walked he knew not whither. He found himself, he knew not how, on the bank of the river. Seizing an old board for a paddle, he unloosed a skiff and pushed out into the river. How to advance himself over his rival was his first thought. But this darkness and this beating rain and this fierce loneliness, reminded him of that night when he had clung desperately to the abutment of the bridge that spanned Indian Creek, and when the courage and self-possession of Henry Stevens had rescued him. Could he be the rival of a man who had gone down into that flood that he might save the exhausted Marquis?

Then he hated himself. Why had he not drowned that night on Indian Creek? And with this feeling of self-disgust added to his general mental misery, and the physical misery that the rain brought to him, there came the great temptation to write "*Fin*" in French fashion, by jumping into the water. But something in the influence of Priscilla and that class meeting caused him to take a better resolution, and he returned to the hotel.

The next day he sent for Henry Stevens to come to his room.

"Henry, I am going to leave to-night on the mail boat. I am going back to New Orleans, and thence to France. You love Priscilla. You are a noble man; you will make her happy. I have read your love in your face. Meet me at the river to-night. When you are ready to be married, let me know, that I may send some token of my love for both. Do not tell mademoiselle that I am going; but tell her good-bye for me afterwards. Go now, I must pack."

Henry went out stupefied. What did it mean? And why was he half-glad that d'Entremont was going? By degrees he got the better of his selfishness. In fact, he had the habit of keeping his selfishness under in little things, so that the victory in a great thing was not so difficult.

"Marquis d'Entremont," he said, breaking into his room, "you must not go away. You love Priscilla. You have everything—learning, money, travel. I have nothing."

"Nothing but a good heart, which I have not," said d'Entremont.

"I will never marry Priscilla," said Henry, "unless she deliberately chooses to have me in preference to you."

My readers will say that this incident, of two men unselfish in an affair of this sort, is impossible. I should never have written it but that this incident is fact.

To this arrangement, so equitable, the Marquis consented, and the matter was submitted to Priscilla by letter. Could she love either, and if either, which? She asked a week for deliberation.

It was not easy to decide. By all her habits of thought and feeling, by all her prejudices, by all her religious life, she was drawn toward the peaceful and perhaps prosperous life that opened before her as the wife of Henry Stevens, living in her native village, near to her mother, surrounded by her old friends, and with the best of Christian men for a husband. But by all the clamor of her intellectual nature for something better than her narrow life—by all her joy in the conversation of d'Entremont, the only man her equal in culture she had ever known, she felt drawn to be the wife of the Marquis. But if there were roses, there were thorns in such a path. The village girl knew that *Madame la Marquise* must lead a life very different from any she had known. She must bear with a husband whose mind was ever in a state of unrest and scepticism, and she must meet the great world.

In truth there were two Priscillas. There was the Priscilla that her neighbors knew, the Priscilla that went to church, the Priscilla that taught Primary School No. 3. There was the other Priscilla that read Chaucer and Shakspeare, Molière and De Staël. With this Priscilla, New Geneva had nothing to do. And it was the doubleness of her nature that aggravated her indecision.,

Then her conscience came in. Because there might be worldly attractions on the one side, she leaned to the other. To reject a poor suitor and accept a rich and titled one, had something of treason in it.

At the end of a week she sent for them both. Henry Stevens' flat-boat had been ready to start for New Orleans for two days. And Challeau, Lafort & Cie. were expecting the Marquis, who was in some sort a ward of theirs. Henry Stevens and the Marquis Antoine d'Entremont walked side by side, in an awkward silence, to the little vine-covered cottage. Of that interview I do not know enough to write fully. But I know that Priscilla said such words as these : —

"This is an awful responsibility. I suppose a judge trembles when he must pass sentence of death. But I must make a decision that involves the happiness of both my friends and myself. I cannot do it now. God does not give me to see my duty clearly, and nothing but duty should speak in making such a decision. Will you wait until you both return in the spring? I have a reason that I cannot explain for wishing this matter postponed. God will decide for me, perhaps."

I do not know that she said just these words; and I know she did not say them at all once. But so they parted. And Miss Nancy More, who retailed ribbons and scandal, and

whose only effort at mental improvement had been the pluck-
ing out of the hairs contiguous to her forehead, that she might
look intellectual, — Miss Nancy More from her look-out at the
window descried the two friends walking away from Mrs.
Haines' cottage, and remarked, as she had often remarked
before, that it was "absolutely scandalous for a young woman
who was a professor to have two beaux at once, and such
good friends, too ! "

I have noticed that gifted girls like Priscilla have a back-
ground in some friend, intelligent, quiet, restful. Anna Poindexter, a dark, thoughtful, and altogether excellent girl, was
sometimes spoken of as "Priscilla's double;" but she was
rather Priscilla's opposite : all her gifts were complementary
to those of her friend. The two were all but inseparable ; and
so, when Priscilla found herself the next evening on the bank
of the river, she naturally found Anna with her. Slowly the
flat-boat, of which Henry Stevens was owner and captain,
drifted by, while the three or four men at each long oar strode
back and forward on the deck as they urged the boat on.
Henry was standing on the elevated bench made for the pilot,
holding the long "steering-oar" and guiding the craft. As his
manly form in the western sunlight attracted their attention,
both the girls were struck with admiration for the noble fellow.
Both waved their handkerchiefs, and Henry returned the adieu
by swinging his hat. So intent was he on watching them that
he forgot his duty, and one of the men was obliged to call out,
"Swing her round, captain, or the mail-boat 'll sink us."

Hardly was the boat swung out of the way when the tall-
chimneyed mail-boat swept by.

"See the Marquis," cried Anna, and again adieux were
waved ; and the Marquis stepped to the guard and called out
to Henry, "I'll see you in New Orleans ;" and the swift steamer
immediately bore him out of speaking distance. And Henry

watched him disappear, with a choking feeling that thus the nobleman was to outstrip him in life.

"See!" said Anna, "you are a lucky girl. You have your choice: you can go through life on the steamboat or on the flat-boat. Of course you'll go by steam."

"There are explosions on steamboats sometimes," said Priscilla. Then turning, she noticed a singular expression on Anna's face. Her insight was quick, and she said, "Confess that *you* would choose the flat-boat." And Anna turned away.

"Two strings to her bow, or two beaux to her string, I should say," and she did say it; for this was Miss More's comment on the fact which she had just learned, that Miss Haines had received letters from "the lower country," the handwriting on the directions of which indicated that she had advices from both her friends. But poor Miss More, with never a string to her bow, and never a beau to her string, might be forgiven for shooting arrows that did no harm.

There was a time when Priscilla had letters from only one. Henry was very sick, and d'Entremont wrote bulletins of his condition to Priscilla and to his family. In one of these it was announced that he was beyond recovery, and Priscilla and Anna mingled their tears together. Then there came a letter that he was better. Then he was worse again; and then better.

In those days the mail was brought wholly by steamboats, and it took many days for intelligence to come. But the next letter that Priscilla had was from Henry Stevens himself. It was filled from first to last with praises of the Marquis: how he had taken Henry out of his boarding place, put him in his own large room in the St. Charles; how he had nursed him with more than a brother's tenderness, scarcely sleeping at all; how he had sold his cargo, relieved his mind of care, em-

ployed the most eminent physicians, and anticipated his every
want—all this, and more, the letter told.

And the next steamboat brought Henry, wellnigh restored,
and his noble nurse. Both were impatient to learn the decision of Priscilla; each was sure the other was to carry off the
prize.

And so they walked together, the day after their arrival, to
the little cottage. The conversation was begun by each of the
gentlemen expressing his conviction that her decision was
against him, and offering to retire.

Priscilla leaned her head on her hand a minute. Then she
began: "I told you, my friends, that I thought God would
decide for me. He has. I can marry neither of you."

The two friends looked at one another in doubt and amaze-
ment.

"Three sisters, four brothers, and my father died of pul-
monary disease. Of eight children, I only am left, and in
three months my mother will be childless. God has decided
for me. Why should I give either of you pain by making a
decision?"

For the first time, in the imperfect light, they noticed the
flushed cheeks, and for the first time they detected the quick
breathing. It was a sad hour; and when they walked away,
the two friends were nearer than ever, for nothing brings souls
together so much as a common sorrow.

And as day after day the two friends visited her in company, the public, and particularly that part of the public which
peeped out of Miss Nancy More's windows, was not a little
mystified. Miss More thought a girl who was drawing near
to the solemn and awful realities of eternal bliss should let
such worldly vanities as Markusses alone!

A singular change came over Priscilla in one regard. As
the prospect of life faded out, she was no longer in danger of

being tempted by the title and wealth of the Marquis. She could be sure that her heart was not bribed. And when this restraint of a conscience abnormally sensitive was removed, it became every day more and more clear to her that she loved d'Entremont. Of all whom she had ever known, he was a companion. And as he brought her choice passages from favorite writers every day, and as her mind grew with unwonted rapidity under the influence of that strange disease which shakes the body down while it ripens the soul, she felt more and more that she was growing out of sympathy with all that was narrow and provincial in her former life, and into sympathy with God's great world, and with Antoine d'Entremont, who was the representative of the world to her.

This rapidly growing gulf between his own intellectual life and that of Priscilla, Henry Stevens felt keenly. But there is one great compensation for a soul like Henry's. Men and women of greater gifts might outstrip him in intellectual growth. He could not add one cell to his brain, or make the slightest change in his temperament. But neither the Marquis nor Priscilla could excel him in that gift of noble generosity which does not always go with genius, and which is not denied to the man of the plainest gifts. He wrote to the Marquis : —

"My Dear Friend : — You are a good and generous friend. I have read in her voice and her eyes what the decision of Priscilla must have been. If I had not been blind, I ought to have seen it before in the difference between us. Now I know that it will be a comfort to you to have that noble woman die your wife. I doubt not it will be a comfort to her. Do you think it will be any consolation to me to have been an obstacle in the way? I hope you do not think so meanly of me, and that you and Priscilla will give me the only consolation I can have in our common sorrow — the feeling that I have been able to make her last days more comfortable and your sorrow more bearable. If you refuse, I shall always reproach myself. Henry."

I need not tell of the discussions that ensued. But it was

concluded that it was best for all three that Priscilla and the Marquis should be married, much to the disgust of Miss Nancy More, who thought that "she'd better be sayin' her prayers. What good would it do to be a Marchoness, and all that, when she was in her coffin?"

A wedding in prospect of death is more affecting than a funeral. Only Henry Stevens and Anna Poindexter were to be present. Priscilla's mother had completed the arrangements, blinded by tears. I think she could have dressed Priscilla for her coffin with less suffering. The white dress looked so like a shroud, under those sunken cheeks as white as the dress! Once or twice Priscilla had drawn her mother's head to her bosom and wept.

"Poor mother!" she would say, "so soon to be alone. But Antoine will be your son."

There was one more at the wedding than was intended. The family physician was there; for, just as the dressing of the pale bride was completed, there came one of those sudden breakdowns to which a consumptive is so liable. The doctor said that there was internal hemorrhage, and gave but a few hours of life. When the Marquis came he was heart-broken to see her lying there, so still, so white — dying. She took his hand. She beckoned to Anna and Henry Stevens to stand by her, and then, with tear-blinded eyes, the old minister married them for eternity! Then the door opened, and the ten little Sunday-school boys from Slabtown marched in. Each of them had a bouquet provided by Henry Stevens for the wedding. When the leader of the file saw her so sick he began to cry. She took his bouquet and kissed him. Then the little fellow rushed out, weeping piteously. Each of the others followed his example.

Feeling life ebbing, she took the hand of the Marquis. Then, holding to the hand of d'Entremont, she beckoned

Henry to come near. As he bent over her she said, looking significantly at the Marquis, "Henry, God bless you, my noble-hearted friend!" and as Henry turned away, the Marquis put his arm about him and said gratefully, "Henry, God *will* bless you."

Priscilla's nature abhorred anything dramatic in dying, or rather she did not think of effect at all; so she made no fine speeches. But when she had ceased to breathe, the old preacher said, "The bridegroom has come." And he was more eloquent than he knew.

She left an envelope for Henry. What it had in it no one but Henry ever knew. I have heard him say that it was one word, which became the key to all the happiness of his after life. Judging from the happiness he has in his home with Anna, his wife, it would not be hard to tell what the word was. The last time I was at his house I noticed that their eldest child was named Priscilla, and that the boy who came next was Antoine. Henry told me that Priscilla left a sort of "will" for the Marquis, in which she asked him to do the Christian work that she would have liked to do. Nothing could have been wiser if she had only sought his own happiness, for in activity for others is the only safety for a restless and sceptical mind. He had made himself the special protector of the ten little Slabtown urchins.

Henry told me in how many ways, through Challeau, La-fort & Cie., the Marquis had contrived to contribute to his prosperity without offending his delicacy. He found himself possessed of practically unlimited credit through the guarantee which the great New Orleans banking-house was always ready to give.

"What is that fine building?" I said, pointing to a picture on the wall.

"Oh, that is the 'Hospice de Sainte Priscille,' which Antoine has erected in Paris. People there call it 'La Marquise.'"

"By the way," said Priscilla's mother, who sat by, "Antoine is coming to see us next month, and is to look after his Slab-town friends when he comes. They used to call him at first 'Priscilla's Frenchman.'"

And to this day Miss More declares that Markusses is a thing she can't noways understand.

91

IN MEMORIAM.

In Memoriam.

JOHN A. ANDREW.

WRITTEN FOR THE DEDICATION OF THE STATUE OF GOV. ANDREW,
AT HINGHAM, MASS., OCT. 9, 1875.

BY OLIVER WENDELL HOLMES.

BEHOLD the shape our eyes have known!
It lives once more in changeless stone:
So looked in mortal face and form
Our guide through peril's deadly storm.

But hushed the beating heart we knew,
That heart so tender, brave and true,
Firm as the rooted mountain rock,
Pure as the quarry's whitest block!

Not his beneath the blood-red star
To win the soldier's envied scar:
Unarmed he battled for the right,
In Duty's never-ending fight.

Unconquered will, unslumbering eye,
Faith such as bids the martyr die,
The prophet's glance, the master's hand
To mould the work his foresight planned.

These were his gifts; what Heaven had lent
For justice, mercy, truth, he spent,
First to avenge the traitorous blow,
And first to lift the vanquished foe.

Lo, thus he stood; in danger's strait
The pilot of the Pilgrim State!
Too large his fame for her alone, —
A nation claims him as her own!

95

THE WATER! THE WATER!

THE WATER! THE WATER!

BY WILLIAM MOTHERWELL.

THE Water! The Water!
  The joyous brook for me,
That tuneth through the quiet night
  Its ever-living glee.
The Water! The Water!
  That sleepless, merry heart,
Which gurgles on unstintedly,
  And loveth to impart,
To all around it, some small measure
Of its own most perfect pleasure.

The Water! The Water!
  The gentle stream for me,
That gushes from the old gray stone
  Beside the alder-tree.
The Water! The Water!
  That ever-bubbling spring
I loved and looked on, while a child,
  In deepest wondering,
And asked it whence it came and went,
And when its treasures would be spent.

The Water! The Water!
  My heart yet burns to think
How cool thy fountain sparkled forth
  For parched lip to drink.
The Water! The Water!
  Of mine own native glen, —
The gladsome tongue I oft have heard,
  But ne'er shall hear again,
Though fancy fills my ear for aye
With sounds that live so far away!

The Water!   The Water!
  The mild and glassy wave,
Upon whose broomy banks I've longed
  To find my silent grave.
The Water!   The Water!
  Oh, blest to me thou art,
Thus sounding in life's solitude
  The music of my heart,
And filling it, despite of sadness,
With dreamings of departed gladness.

The Water!   The Water!
  The mournful, pensive tone
That whispered to my heart how soon
  This weary life was done.
The Water!   The Water!
  That rolled so bright and free,
And bade me mark how beautiful
  Was its soul's purity,
And how it glanced to heaven its wave,
As, wandering on, it sought its grave.

OLD RUDDERFORD HALL.

OLD RUDDERFORD HALL.

BY MISS M. E. BRADDON,

Author of "Lady Audley's Secret," "Aurora Floyd," "Birds of Prey," etc., etc.

————— ◆◆◆ —————

CHAPTER I.

LD RUDDERFORD HALL lay back from the high road, buried in trees, and all the traveller saw of it was a glimpse of mellow, red-brick chimney, or an angle of the steep-tiled roof, above oaks and elms that had been growing ever since the Norman Conquest, when all about the trim little out-of-the-world village of Rudderford was forest land.

New Rudderford Hall fronted the turnpike road, resplendent with three rows of shining plate-glass windows, a brilliant stuccoed front, a conservatory with a glass dome flashing in the summer sun, a prim lawn embellished with geometrical flower-beds, all ablaze with scarlet and yellow, and two pair of bran-new Birmingham iron gates, of florid design, surmounted by two pair of lamps. New Rudderford Hall looked what it was — the abode of commercial wealth. New Rudderford Hall gave dinner parties, a ball once a year, hunting breakfasts in the late autumn, private theatricals at Christmas. New Rudderford Hall had three rosy daughters and one stalwart, hard-riding son, the apple of its eye.

Old Rudderford Hall rarely opened its rusty gates or unlocked its creaking doors. There was, indeed, a legend that no stranger had broken bread there for a century; yet there was a counter-story current to the effect that the master of Old Rudderford Hall could, when he chose, open a bottle of rare old wine for a visitor, — Madeira that had voyaged three times to and fro the East Indies, sirupy Malmsey, golden-tinted Tokay, oily Constantia, with a faint bitter twang. Old Rudderford Hall had one only child, a daughter, fair to see, who rode an ancient purblind palfrey about the shady lanes round Rudderford, and was met sometimes in the dwellings of the poor, but never in that exalted sphere, which Rudderford called " society." Old Rudderford Hall rejoiced in that patrician appendage, — a family ghost.

The story went that a Champion of the days of the Stuarts had slain his wife in some fit of jealous fury, and that the poor lady's restless spirit — the legend hinted at her guilt — haunted the long, dark passages and dismal chambers of the old house. It was not very clear that any one had ever seen her, but she was firmly believed in, nevertheless, and plenty of people were able to give a graphic description of her, — a tall, graceful lady, dressed in white, with flowing auburn hair falling over her neck and shoulders.

The present owner of the Hall was Anthony Champion, and the estate had belonged to the house of Champion ever since the days of Henry VIII., who, in the distribution of church property, had rewarded his liege servant, Thomas Champion, gentleman, for divers services not set down in the title-deeds of the estate, with the copyhold of Rudderford Chase and Rudderford Grange, previously held by a monkish fraternity settled in the neighborhood.

There were portions of the old Grange still standing, — massive stone walls pierced with narrow, arched windows, a winding staircase, and low, oak door, iron-bound and studded with huge nails; but these stone buildings now served only as offices, and the Hall proper had been built by the aforesaid Thomas Champion, with much splendor and lavish expenditure, in an age when architectural extravagance had been made fashionable by the magnificent Wolsey. The house was one of the finest specimens of domestic architecture in England, but had been sorely neglected for the last century. Wherever decay could arise, it had arisen, and a settled gloom had fallen upon the mansion and its surroundings. Only in the flower-garden was there any glimpse of neatness or brightness, and that was due to the care of Christabel Champion, who loved the old flower-beds, the grassy walks, and ancient roses, and who not only superintended the labors of a great hulking lad of seventeen, sole gardener at the Hall, but worked hard herself into the bargain.

Within, the gloom was almost oppressive. Anthony Champion was a man who lived amongst his books, and dreamed away his days over mouldy old folios and rare editions collected by his father, when the Champion purse was deeper than it was nowadays. He lived almost wholly in his library, only emerging at seven in the evening to share his daughter's frugal dinner, and to doze or muse for an hour or so afterwards in the long saloon. There was some little show of state and ceremony kept up at the Hall, though there were only three servants in a house where there had once been forty — an ancient butler and housekeeper, man and wife, and a buxom country girl, who did all the scrubbing and cleaning, attended to a small dairy, and waited upon Christabel.

The master of Old Rudderford Hall was as poor as Job in his day of affliction; or at least so ran the common rumor, amply sustained by the mode and manner of his existence. A hundred years ago there had been revelry and splendor at the grand old house, but at that time a great misfortune befel its master, in the untimely death of his eldest son, killed in a duel; and the bereaved father shut up the house, and went to France, where he lived a wild life, and squandered a noble fortune at the profligate court of Louis the Well-beloved. He died in Paris a year or so before the revolution, which was to regenerate mankind, arrived at that stage in which it began to improve them off the face of the earth, and probably by his timely decease escaped a ruder exit *via* the guillotine. His estate, much impoverished, descended to a nephew, a studious young man, lame and of feeble health, who married a girl of humble birth, lived the life of a recluse in the neglected house, and became the father of Anthony Champion, the present master of the old Hall.

It is possible that, when young Anthony inherited the estate, shrunk and burdened as it was, he might have made some effort to brighten and improve things, if fortune had favored him ever so little. But again did affliction fall heavily upon the old house. He married a woman he adored, a fair young girl of high family but no fortune, and brought her home to the Hall, full of all manner of schemes for the future. For a little more than a year he lived a life of supreme domestic happiness, and then — two months after the birth of a baby-girl — he saw an unusual flush upon his young wife's cheek one day, and the next beheld her stricken with typhus-fever. In a week all was over, and he stood alone by his dreary hearth, like a strong man turned to stone. It was long before the caresses of his child could bring the faintest shadow of a smile to his haggard face. He seemed to grow an old man all at once. Unlike his ancestor, he did not turn his back upon the scene of his suffering; he only entombed himself there, buried alive among his books. He had inherited his father's studious habits; and after a weary year, in which he sat alone day after day, helpless, hopeless, blankly staring at the wall before him, and brooding over his misery, he grew to find some cold comfort in recondite studies of so close and severe a kind, that the more credulous among his neighbors talked darkly as of something not quite canny.

For such a man society could have no charm. Had he possessed the wealth of all the Rothschilds, he would have lived very much as he did live. A retinue of servants might have eaten and drunk at his expense, a vast amount of splendid upholstery might have been created at his cost; but his individual expenditure would have been no greater, his manner of existence no more cheerful. He lived alone by choice; and so utterly narrowed had his mind become by constant brooding on one vain regret, as to make him half-unconscious that this hermit life was scarcely the best and brightest for a girl of eighteen. The motherless baby, whose plaintive cries had rent his heart years ago, had blossomed into a lovely girl, painfully like his lost wife. Long and dreary as his days and nights had seemed to him ever since *that* loss, he had been scarcely conscious of the actual progress of time. The lapse might be five years or fifty. It was a surprise to him to see his daughter grown to womanhood. He woke up from a long sleep, as it were, and looked at her with vague wonder. Seven or eight years before, he had made a friendly arrangement with the rector's wife, by which Christabel was to share the studies of the four girls at the rectory, under an admirable governess; and by virtue of this arrangement his daughter's education had cost him very little money and no trouble.

He loved her fondly, and yet had given her little of his confidence. Rarely did he see the fair young face looking up at him without a faint pang, which was like the memory of an acute agony rather than actual present pain. She was so like her mother! He fancied sometimes how fair a picture those two faces would have made side by side — one developed and matronly, the other in all the bloom of girlhood.

She had her little circle of friends — a very small one. The only house she visited was the rectory, and there she came and went like a daughter of the house. There she had met the New

Rudderford Hall people — Frank Greenwood and his three sisters, who fell in love with her — the sisters, that is to say — at first sight. Frank said very little about her. She declined all invitations for parties, however — indeed, she had none of the finery required for such occasions — but consented to join them now and then on the croquet-lawn and share their afternoon tea.

CHAPTER II.

EW RUDDERFORD HALL was built upon a part of the land which King Henry bestowed upon his liege Thomas Champion, and this fact was resented by Anthony as a personal offence against him upon the part of Mr. Greenwood. If he had been a visiting man even, nothing could have induced him to break bread with the master of the new Hall, and he always heard of his daughter's intimacy with "those Greenwood girls" with displeasure.

"I can't imagine what induces you to cultivate such people, Christabel," he said fretfully, as they were sitting together in the summer dusk after dinner one evening in the long saloon — a melancholy room which would have accommodated an assembly of fifty, and seemed very dreary in its faded splendor, occupied only by the father and daughter.

"I never have cultivated them, papa. You know how many invitations they have sent me, and I have declined them all."

"You have been to their house."

"Yes, to play croquet, now and then; never to any of their parties."

"I suppose that is a deprivation," said Mr. Champion, with a sigh. "I daresay there are people who would call me a cruel father, and the life you lead in this old house an unnatural one."

"Pray, pray don't say that, my dear father," cried the girl earnestly, coming over to his chair by the open window, and laying her hand caressingly upon his shoulder. "You know that I am quite content to be with you; there is no higher happiness I could desire than that. If our lives are a little dull sometimes, and one is subject to an occasional attack of low spirits, never mind; there are other times when life seems all sunshine, and the garden and the dear old house enchanted, like the fairy palace in *Beauty and the Beast*. Why, after all, my life is quite as gay as Beauty's was. As long as you like to live alone, papa, I will be content with our solitude; though I confess it would make me happy to see you go more into the world."

The world, in Christabel's ideas, meant Rudderford and half-a-dozen houses within half-a-dozen miles of Rudderford. Perhaps the world of which she was thinking just at this moment meant even something less than that—an occasional dinner-party at Samuel Greenwood's smart stuccoed mansion.

"That is a sight you will never see, my dear," answered her father drearily. "I shut my door upon the world when I came home from your mother's funeral—home! and she was no longer there! No, Christabel; the world and I have parted company too long for any sympathy to be possible between us. A man coming out into the clamor and confusion of Paris after five-and-twenty years in one of the underground cells of the Bastille could not feel himself more a stranger than I should, if I were to go into the world now. But I am not going to keep you buried alive forever. You have blossomed into a woman all at once, and taken me by surprise. I want a little time to think about it, and then I shall form some plan for giving you a brighter life."

"I don't wish for any change, papa; I would not leave you. If you have any plan for sending me away, pray abandon it.

Not all the pleasures in the world would make up to me for leaving you. Indeed, indeed, I am quite happy! I have my poor people to visit, and — and — a few friends " — she hesitated, with a sudden blush, remembering that those obnoxious Greenwoods were among the few — " and my dear old horse, Gilpin."

Mr. Champion smiled at the mention of this last item.

" Gilpin is scarcely a steed for a young lady to boast of," said he. " I suppose the world thinks that I can give you no better mount than old Gilpin; that I live the life I do from poverty as much as for any other reason."

" People may think so, papa; what does it matter? "

" Nothing, child; but for once the world is out in its reckoning. I am not a poor man. The estate was heavily burdened when I succeeded to it, but money has accumulated rapidly in the life I have led, and I have paid off everything, — have saved money, too. If I could have only bought back the land upon which the new hall stands, and pulled down that vulgar cockney house, I should think my money worth something; but that's out of the question. Samuel Greenwood is one of the richest men in the county, and would dearly like to buy me out of this place. However, don't let's talk of him; the subject always puts me out of temper. When the time comes for your marrying, Christabel, you will not be a penniless bride."

" I hope, if ever I do marry, papa, it will be some one who won't care whether I have any money or not."

" Of course; that's a girl's notion. But people do care. I don't want you to marry a pauper, who, having nothing to bestow, would be content to take you with nothing. The age has grown commercial, my dear; the more money a man has, the more he expects with his wife. And when you go into society by and by, as I intend you shall do, you shall appear as becomes a gentleman's daughter; and when you marry, you shall have such jewels as not one woman in a hundred can show."

" Jewels, papa ! " cried Christabel, opening her blue eyes to their widest extent, — " jewels."

Except a white cornelian necklace and a gold heart-shaped locket containing her mother's hair, the girl had never possessed a trinket in her life.

" Yes, child, jewels. Stay here a minute, and I'll show you something."

There was a door at one end of the saloon opening into the library, that darksome den in which Anthony Champion spent his days, and which was rarely invaded by the foot of the industrious housemaid. A dingy old room, lined from floor to ceiling with dingy books, — books in piles on the floor, books on the mantelpiece, books heaped up on the three broad, oak window-seats, books everywhere, and between the windows two huge carved-oak muniment chests.

Anthony left his daughter in the saloon, and went into the library. He unlocked one of these muniment chests, and took out a battered old leather-covered box, which had once been crimson. This he brought to Christabel. There was just light enough for her to see some faded gilt lettering at the top, — the initials " C. C."

" Was that my mother's? " she asked, scrutinizing those two letters with interest.

" No. This jewel-case belonged to your great-aunt, Caroline Champion, the mother of that unhappy lad who lost his life in a drunken brawl which ended in bloodshed. When Angus Champion turned his back upon Rudderford, he left this box behind him, — forgot its existence, perhaps ; who knows ? His wife had been dead nine years. At any rate, although he spent almost everything he could lay his hands on, the jewels remained in an iron safe in the steward's room, among old leases and useless parchments, and there my father found them when he inherited the property. As they had escaped so long, he did not

111

care to sell them. 'My son's wife shall wear them,' he said. But your mother never lived to wear them, Christabel. We used to talk merrily enough of the day when she should be presented at court, in a blaze of diamonds. Yet she wore no ornaments but the roses we put in her coffin." He stopped for a few moments; *that* memory never came to him without the familiar pang. "And now I am going to dazzle your eyes," he said, putting aside the bitter thought with an effort. There are loves that do verily last a lifetime, and his was one of those.

He unlocked the jewel-case, and lifted the lid. Christabel gave a great cry of rapture. There was a tray of diamonds, — necklace, bracelets, brooch, ear-rings, set in silver, in a solid, simple style. The stones were large and brilliant, perfect in color, of a greater value than Anthony Champion imagined, though he deemed them worth a round sum.

He raised the upper tray, and revealed a lower one, full of sapphires, in a quaint filigree gold setting; then he showed his daughter another tray, containing a necklace and ear-rings of amethysts and pearls, which Christabel declared were more beautiful than the diamonds; and then the bottom of the box, in which there were only odds and ends, — antique rings, an apostle's spoon, a smelling-bottle, a couple of thimbles, a fruit-knife, a locket, a brooch or two, and so on. But these interested Christabel almost more than the precious stones, and she sat looking them over entranced, with the three jewel-trays spread out upon the table.

"Hark!" said her father suddenly. "What was that?"

"What, papa?"

"That noise outside; it sounded like a step upon the gravel Look out, Christabel, and see if there is any one."

Miss Champion stepped out of the long window. There was a wide gravel walk before the saloon windows, somewhat weedy and moss-grown, and beyond that a shrubbery, where the young firs and shrubs grew thick and tall, — a shrubbery in which a dozen men might have hidden securely enough.

There was no one to be seen. The girl glanced up and down the weedy walk, very desolate-looking in the summer twilight, and peered into the shrubbery, parting the thick laurels here and there, but without result.

" Are you sure you heard a footstep, papa ? " she asked, rather incredulously, as she came back to the room.

" Yes," said Mr. Champion, who had been hastily replacing the jewel-trays, while his daughter was looking about, " I am sure. And there was something more than a footstep. I saw a shadow fall across the window."

" The shadow of a tree, perhaps, papa."

" There is no tree that can cast a shadow on this window. It was gone in a moment. There has been some one watching us, Christabel."

" A tramp, perhaps, papa," said Miss Champion, coolly.

The approaches to old Rudderford Hall were ill guarded, — guarded not at all, in fact. The gates were never locked, and for those intruders who might find the legitimate mode of entrance inconvenient, there were numerous gaps in the fence through which they might roam into the park at will.

Plenty of tramps, therefore, came to the old hall, and were wont to depart, protesting against the inhospitality of the back door and kitchen department in general. There were no beer-drinking grooms to wheedle out of a friendly pint; no gossiping scullerymaids to give them bread and cheese or broken victuals, — the bone of a leg of mutton and half a loaf of bread, or the carcasses of a pair of fowls and a dish of cold vegetables. There was nothing to be heard or seen, no hen-roosts to be robbed, — for the poultry-yard was a desert: only close-shut doors, and blank iron-barred windows; weeds growing between the flagstones in the court, an empty dog-kennel, a locked dairy, a broken pump, which would not yield the wanderer so much as the refreshment of a draught of spring water.

"A tramp!" exclaimed Mr. Champion, with displeasure. "I'm afraid you encourage such vermin by your indiscriminate charities, Christabel."

Christabel looked downward with a faint little sigh. If not a miser in theory, Mr. Champion had been a miser in practice; and so restricted was her pocket-money, that these indiscriminate charities of which he complained consisted of a stray sixpence now and then bestowed upon some footsore vagrant, whose piteous tale touched the tender young heart.

"A tramp!" repeated Mr. Champion; "a pleasant thing for a tramp to have seen those jewels. I'll put them away this moment, and do you look out again, Christabel, and see if you can discover any one lurking about; and you might tell David to keep his eyes open."

David was the solitary gardener and out-of-door-man, who had the custody of grounds that could have been barely kept in order by six.

Miss Champion stepped out into the garden again under a darkening sky, and this time looked more closely than before, making a circuit of the shrubbery by a path half choked with the wild growth of neglected shrubs, going round into the old Dutch garden, glancing even into the kitchen garden beyond, where she found David staring pensively into a broken cucumber frame.

To him she gave her father's order, which he received almost contemptuously.

"Tramps, miss! Lor' a mercy, they don't do no harm There's nothing for 'em to steal."

Of course the intruder, whoever he might be, must have had ample time to make his escape after Mr. Champion first took alarm. David prowled slowly through the gardens, stared

114

across a massive holly hedge into the park, saw no one, and wended his solitary way to the house to report accordingly.

———

CHAPTER III.

HRISTABEL met Rosa Greenwood next morning in one of the green lanes beyond the village when she was returning from a long ramble on Gilpin, and that young lady told her of a croquet party that was to take place at New Rudderford Hall that evening, and to which she must certainly come.

"It's not the least bit in the world a party, you know, dear," Miss Greenwood pleaded, patting Gilpin's iron-gray shoulder; "quite an impromptu affair, got up for Miss Perkington, only daughter of the great firm of Perkington and Tanberry, cloth manufacturers, who is staying with us. *Such* a dear girl! not exactly pretty, but *so* interesting. We all want Frank to marry her, and I really think she likes him. But there's no knowing; young men are so peculiar."

Christabel wore a straw hat with a blue veil, and under the blue veil the roses on her cheeks deepened a little at this juncture.

"Now you must, must, must come, Christabel. I won't accept a refusal. The rectory girls are to be with us. We are to dine at five, so as to secure a long evening, and begin croquet at six; and we can wind up with a waltz or two before supper."

Christabel's eyes quite sparkled at the idea of a waltz. Dancing was a dissipation which seemed to her inexperience the height of earthly felicity. She had waltzed all by herself on the lawn many a summer evening, softly singing some languorous melody of D'Albert's as she danced.

" I should dearly like to come," she said thoughtfully, " but I don't know if papa — "

" Papa! bosh!" exclaimed Miss Greenwood, who was somewhat fast and irreverent in her notions of parental authority. " I should like to see the author of *my* being putting a spoke in the wheel if I wanted to enjoy myself. As if your life wasn't dull enough, mewed up in that dreary old Hall!" And Miss Greenwood made a wry face, which expressed her supreme contempt for the grand old Tudor mansion, as compared with the smart plate-glass-windowed habitation which sheltered her fair self.

" I'll ask papa if I may come at eight," said Christabel. " He dines at seven, you know, and he always likes to have me with him at dinner. I couldn't possibly come *till* eight; but the evenings are so long now."

" It's a great deal too late," replied Rosa, picking a fly off Gilpin's nose. " However, if you must stop to see that curious old pa of yours eat his dinner, you must. But remember, we shall expect you at eight sharp. I'll send Frank to meet you at the field gate."

" Oh, please don't," cried Christabel.

" But I please shall. He'll meet you at the gate when the clock strikes eight."

Miss Champion walked her horse to the end of the lane, Rosa Greenwood walking by her side, telling her about that wonderful young person Miss Victoria Perkington, who, by virtue of her position as the only daughter of Perkington and Tanberry, had an allowance which made the condition of the rich Miss Greenwoods seem absolute penury.

" You should see the dresses she has brought with her for a ten days' visit!" exclaimed Rosa. " A basket as big as a house, and all of them from a Frenchwoman in Bruton street. There's a corded black silk trimmed with white lace — Valenciennes — three inches deep on all the flounces and puffings; worth a fortune — a perfect duck of a dress!"

Christabel thought of her jewels, and wished that she could have melted just a few diamonds, which she could never wear till she was married, into silk dresses. She gave a little sigh, thinking of the scantiness of her wardrobe, and how very poor a figure she must needs seem in the eyes of Miss Perkington, and rode slowly home, meditative, and not altogether happy.

"I dare say he will marry her," she said to herself. "It is just as papa said last night. The richer people are, the more eager they are to increase their wealth. He will marry her, no doubt, and buy some great estate in the neighborhood, and build a big, ugly house; and I shall see them riding by on their thorough-bred horses, and laughing at poor old Gilpin."

She bent over her horse's neck to pat him at this thought, and one childish tear dropped upon the gray mane. She was not much more than a child, and Frank Greenwood had been very tender and deferential in his manner to her always. It gave her a sharp pain to think that he would pass quite out of her life, and belong to Miss Perkington.

"Would you object to my going to play croquet at — at the new Hall this evening, papa?" the girl asked timidly, during dinner.

"Object? Well, my dear, you know I detest those Greenwood people," — it is doubtful if he had seen them three times in his life, — "but I suppose it would be hard upon you to forbid your enjoying any little pleasure they may offer you in a quiet way. It is not a party, of course?"

"Oh, no, papa. I only heard of it from Rosa when I was out this morning."

"Mind, I set my face absolutely against your appearance at any of their ostentatious parties. I'll not have *my* daughter paraded at Joshua Greenwood's chariot-wheels. But as far as a game of croquet goes, if it pleases you, I've no objection."

" Thanks, dear papa."

" When are you going?"

" Directly after dinner."

" That will be at eight o'clock. I shall send David for you at half-past nine."

Only an hour and a half! Would there be time for those waltzes on the lawn? She had danced several times with Frank at that hospitable rectory, and knew that he was an agreeable partner.

"There is to be a kind of supper, I believe, papa," she faltered.

" A kind of supper? Say ten, then, or half-past at the latest."

" Thank you, papa dear."

" Bless my heart! one would think these people were the most congenial acquaintance you could desire."

" The rectory girls are to be there, papa," Christabel said demurely.

" Well, I don't wonder at your being attached to *them*. Run away, child, and dress yourself. I can finish my dinner alone."

Miss Champion kissed her father, and tripped away to make her brief toilet; pleased, and yet with a vague pain at her heart — a pain that was associated with the image of the unknown Miss Perkington. Rosa Greenwood had called her brother "peculiar" in a tone that seemed to imply his indifference to the great heiress; but she had not said the marriage was at all unlikely; and the family wished it; and Miss Perkington was *there;* and Frank was a man of the world — very bright, and clever, and open-hearted, but a man of the world nevertheless.

She put on her white muslin dress, — a dress three summers old, which had been lengthened artfully, but not quite imperceptibly, to suit her increasing height; just such a dress as

118

must of necessity provoke contempt in the mind of Miss Perkington, who of course had never in her life worn anything lengthened, or "let out." She tied a broad blue ribbon round her slim white throat, with the gold heart-shaped locket hanging to it, and then looked at herself in the glass discontentedly. It was a very beautiful picture which she saw in that old-fashioned cheval glass — a tall, slender, white-robed figure, and a fair young face framed in luxuriant auburn hair; but Christabel only saw the deficiencies of her costume, and turned away from the glass with a sigh.

Her father was dozing in his deep arm-chair when she peeped into the saloon to bid him good-by; so she went lightly out of the window, and away through the gardens, into a meadow where a solitary cow was browsing in the still evening atmosphere, and on to that field gate of which Miss Greenwood had spoken; a gate that divided Samuel Greenwood's territory from the shrunken lands of the Champions.

Rudderford Church clock chimed the three-quarters after seven as Christabel crossed the meadow. She was just a quarter of an hour before the appointed time. She was half glad, half sorry, to think that Frank would not be there.

He was there, nevertheless — a good-looking young fellow, with long legs, sitting on the gate in a contemplative attitude, thinking so profoundly that he looked up with a start as the light footstep came close to him — a start and something like a blush.

" How good of you to come so early! " he said, as they shook hands, and he held the little hand an extra moment or so. (It was just the sort of meeting in which a young man would consider himself entitled to one gentle pressure before he releases a pretty girl's hand.) " I strolled over here ten minutes ago to have a good think. I don't often think; it's a bad habit."

Christabel laughed. She was almost always gay in his pres

ence; he seemed to brighten her life somehow with a genial influence.

"You must have been obliged to think at Oxford," she said.

Francis Greenwood had taken honors at Oxford a year or so before.

"Not the least in the world. One's tutor does that sort of thing for one. I used to read with a man — a duodecimo edition of Porson in his way, drank like a fish, and knew no end of Greek. When I came to a stiffish passage in Aristotle, I used to throw myself back in my chair and light my cigar. "Just help yourself to another s.-and-b., and be good enough to demonstrate that proposition, old fellow; I don't seem to see it," I used to say; and the dear old bloke would prose away for an hour, and, if I didn't understand it after that, I threw my book at his head and gave it up."

"Was s.-and-b. a dictionary?" Christabel asked naïvely.

"No, Miss Champion, but a wonderful enlightener of the human understanding — soda-water and brandy."

"I'm afraid you led quite a dreadful life at the University."

"Not at all, it was very nice. I should hardly mind leading it over again, only it was not so nice as —."

"As what?" Christabel asked, when he came to a dead stop.

"As the life I hope to lead by and by."

Her heart sank all at once. That meant his life in the big, ugly house that he was to build for himself, and in which he was to set up as a country squire, enriched with the wealth of Perkington and Tanberry. Christabel knew that he was an ardent lover of field-sports, and all pursuits that country gentleman affect, and that he had a vast capacity for spending money. What more natural than that he should be tempted by Miss Perkington's half-million or so?

She was silent. They had one wide meadow to cross, a meadow where the newly-cut grass was fragrant in the still June air, and they would be in the grounds of the new Hall — grounds in which there were very few trees, but a great deal of ornamentation in the way of costly shrubs of divers spikey orders, and winding gravel paths that were kept with rigorous care. They could hear the sharp click of the croquet-balls as they crossed the meadow, and shrill feminine laughter.

" It was very rude of you to leave your side so long," said Christabel.

" My side? Oh, to be sure, those everlasting croquet-players. Do you know, I think croquet the most duffing — I beg your pardon, the most uninteresting game in the world. A man plays it for the sake of loafing with a girl he likes; I can't see any other attraction in it."

" I suppose you have been loafing with Miss Perkington," said Christabel, with a forced little laugh.

Frank Greenwood looked at her curiously.

" Yes," he answered coolly, " I have been loafing with Miss Perkington a good deal lately;" and then he looked at her again.

They were at the iron gate by this time — only a light iron fence divided the grounds from the meadow. Between the lawn and the fence there was that part of the garden called *par excellence* a shrubbery — a scanty grove of the spikey tribe, and young pink hawthorn-trees, as thick in the trunk as a *gandin's* umbrella, and guelder-roses dotted about at intervals — a shrubbery in which there was not covert for a rabbit. Christabel felt that the eyes of all the players on the croquet-ground were upon her, as she traversed the meandering gravel walks with Frank by her side.

The lawn was as smooth and as level as a billiard-table, and there was not so much as a faded leaf among the flower-beds — brilliant pyramids of bloom, rising tier upon tier in rings of contrasting color, or waving in and out in ribbon bordering.

The croquet-ground lay on one side of the house, and scattered around it there were iron seats and tables for the accommodation of loungers and lookers-on. Samuel Greenwood was sitting here, smoking his after-dinner cigar, and reading the "Times;"—a big, bald-headed man, who might once have been like Frank.

He did not look particularly pleased when Christabel came to shake hands with him, smiling shyly, and he gave his son a side-glance that was not altogether agreeable.

"Oh, how d'ye do, Miss Champion?" he said. "I didn't know you were to be here this evening."

"Good gracious me, pa!" exclaimed the irreverent Rosa, "as if we should take the trouble to tell you who was coming to play croquet. Come, Chris, you're to be on our side,—Harry and I" (short for Harriet), "Julia Lee" (the rector's daughter), "and you; Miss Perkington, Frank, Clara Lee, and Patty, on the other side. Now then, first red, get on— Oh, I forgot to introduce you two girls. Miss Perkington, Miss Champion; Miss Champion, Miss Perkington; aristocracy and plutocracy; old Rudderford Hall and the Beeches, Leamington; and now you know all about each other, and I expect you to be good friends immediately."

Miss Perkington bowed stiffly. She did not quite relish such a free-and-easy introduction, but her dear Rosa had such eccentric ways. She was a tall, thin young woman, of an order that is called stylish, with a good many sharp angles, that were artfully toned down by the flouncings and puffings of a French dressmaker; a young woman, with a complexion of the kind that is vulgarly called "tallowy," cold gray eyes, a short, nondescript nose, and a heavy lower jaw. She had good, white teeth, a profusion of black hair, and she held herself well; but it took a large amount of millinery to make Victoria Perkington attractive.

It was not altogether pleasant to Christabel, that game at croquet. In all their previous sport she had had Frank always on her side, achieving wonders by combined dexterity and dishonesty, now boldly pushing her ball to a point of vantage with the toe of his boot, anon calmly pocketing it to avoid the perils of an adversary's croquet; and they had had such fun, such perpetual giggling, such little secrets, and mutual iniquities. This evening they played a rigorous game. Miss Perkington belonged to a croquet-club at Leamington, and would stand no nonsense. She played two hours every afternoon throughout the croquet season, just as regularly as she practised Czerny's exercises on the piano two hours every morning. She had a stroke like a sledge-hammer, and never missed a hoop; so she very soon became a rover, and in that capacity kept a sharp eye upon her ally, Mr. Francis Greenwood. He had not the smallest opportunity for talking to Christabel, even if he had wished to do so, and poor Christabel fancied that he did not wish. He seemed to be upon quite confidential terms with Miss Perkington. He was in fact a young man who could hardly help making himself agreeable to women, and had that semi-flirting manner which some young men cultivate.

Miss Champion played abominably; suffered herself to be croqueted off the face of the earth, as it were, to the extreme indignation of Rosa Greenwood. The Perkington side won with flying colors. Oh, how poor Christabel hated the eau-de-Nil dress, with its innumerable flounces and frillings, the point-lace collar, the Cluny borderings, and all the Perkington caparisons, as that sole daughter of the house of Perkington and Tanberry kept rustling to and fro, sending adverse balls to the farthest limits of space with a cold-blooded ferocity that set Miss Champion's teeth on edge!

When the second game had finished, with dire defeat for Christabel's party, and it was about as dark as ever it is at mid-summer, with the stars shining out one by one from a deep blue sky, Rosa and one of those useful rectory girls went into the drawingroom, and played the famous "Mabel" waltzes. The piano had been wheeled into the bay, and the music floated out through the three tall windows, open from floor to ceiling.

Two of the girls waltzed together, and Frank was still Victoria Perkington's partner. He had scarcely asked her to dance, she had appropriated him as a matter of course.

"If I *am* to dance, I suppose it is to be with you," she said, with her little, supercilious laugh, "since you are our only *danseur*."

She waltzed very well, with all her canvas spread; waltzed too well, Francis Greenwood thought, for he was waiting for her to get tired out in order that he might get just a turn or so with Christabel. She gave him no opportunity for this, however, as she contrived to hold him in conversation — *fade* society talk about people they both knew at Leamington; but, oh, it sounded so confidential, so tender, even, to Christabel's listening ears! — during the pauses in which Miss Perkington condescended to rest, and then went off again like a steam-engine refreshed.

When Frank did at last make his escape, and cross the lawn in quest of Christabel, a shrill voice from the bay-window called out "Supper!" and he was obliged to abandon all hope of that longed-for waltz.

He offered Miss Champion one arm, and gave the other to one of the rectory girls. These were visitors for the evening, and Miss Perkington was staying in the house, and was, in a manner, a member of the family. The fair Victoria rewarded him with a very black look, notwithstanding, when they all came crowding into the brilliantly-lighted dining-room, where Samuel Greenwood sat at the head of his table, with an Aberdeen

salmon *à la mayonnaise* before him, a huge, silvery fish lying in a
bed of greenery, with a bristling hedge of prawns.

"Come here, Victoria, my dear," he said, pointing to the chair
on his right. "Frank, you'll sit next to Miss Perkington; Miss
Lee, you come on my left."

He took no notice of Christabel; but that contumacious
Frank put her coolly into the chair next his own, and so seated
himself between Miss Perkington and her rival.

The heiress of Perkington and Tanberry retired into herself.
Frank tried to divide his attentions between the two girls; but
Miss Perkington only answered him with icy monosyllables, and
pretended to consider all his attempts at general conversation
directed *solely* to Christabel. She scarcely touched her salmon,
declined lobster-salad, would have nothing to say to cold chicken
or pine-apple cream, left the Moselle to waste its fragrance on
the desert air, and sat trifling moodily with half-a-dozen monster
strawberries.

Her ill-temper seemed to communicate itself to Mr. Greenwood, senior, who looked daggers at his son from time to time.
The other girls were uneasy. Christabel, who had brightened
and sparkled into new life at the beginning of the feast, found
out suddenly, in the midst of an animated little discussion, that
she and Frank were the only talkers, and grew silent immediately.

The great ormolu and malachite clock upon the chimney-
piece struck the half-hour after ten.

"Oh, if you please," she whispered to Frank, "I ought to go
away directly, if Mr. Greenwood would not think me rude.
David was to come for me at half-past ten, — the gardener, you
know, — and papa might be angry, if I were to stay later."

"David is a nuisance," said Frank, in his free-and-easy manner;
"though our society is not so entertaining that you need regret
leaving it. I shall see you home, of course."

" Oh, no, pray don't think of that; there's really no occasion."

" There is occasion. You might meet a gang of poachers poaching eggs, or something, and what would David be among so many? There's that fellow they call Black Simeon — the man who got seven years for a burglary at Little Thorpington — has come back to Rudderford. I saw him prowling about the village yesterday, half-seas over. A regular bad lot, that fellow is. Of course I shall come with you. David can walk behind and contemplate the stars. I dare say he knows Orion and the Pleiades as well as that fellow in ' Lockesley Hall," whose knowledge of the heavenly bodies doesn't seem to have been stupendous."

The advent of the indoor man from the rectory, to fetch the Miss Lees, was announced at this moment, so the girls all rose together. A maid who had spirited away Christabel's hat brought it back; and, after a very cool good-night from Joshua Greenwood, who sat scowling at the mutilated salmon, and the stiffest possible bow from Miss Perkington, Miss Champion departed with Frank for her escort.

" Miss Champion has a servant, I believe, Frank," Mr. Greenwood said, sternly.

" I know she has," answered his undutiful son; " but I'm going to see her safe across the meadows, for all that."

Oxford was always too much for Birmingham in any encounter between those two. The commercial magnate had spent three or four thousand pounds upon his son's education, and it seemed to him at odd times that the only tangible produce of that investment was an extensive vocabulary of university slang, and an agreeable placidity of manner which set paternal authority at naught. The young man was not altogether an undutiful son, however, and owned occasionally that his father wasn't " half a bad fellow."

CHAPTER IV.

HE moon had risen while they were losing the calm sweetness of the night in the gas-lit dining-room; the bright full summer moon had risen, and all the spiky trees in the shrubbery were reflected on the smooth grass as if on water, all the flowers in the garden were breathing perfume. Frank and Christabel went out by the drawing-room window, and forgot all about David, who came running after them by and by from the servants' hall, where he had been regaled with beer, and questioned artfully about the " queer ways " of his master. He had to come round by back ways and obscure paths, the gardens being sacred from such vulgar feet as his, and thus did not overtake those two till they were half way across the first meadow. And yet they had dawdled a good deal in the garden, Frank insisting upon picking an especial yellow rose from a standard of his own planting for Christabel.

" You must have one; roses always smell sweeter picked by moonlight," he said. " If you don't find the fact stated in Linnæus, it isn't my fault."

David was a judicious young man. He followed at a respectful distance, and, as Frank had suggested, contemplated, or seemed to contemplate, the sidereal heavens, chewing a twig of hawthorn thoughtfully the while. He allowed an ample margin for loitering at gates, gave Frank so much latitude, in fact, that before they came to the thick wood which made a darkness round Old Rudderford Hall, that undutiful son had asked Christabel to be his wife. Of course, he had set out with no such intention; but the moonlight, and the dewy meadows, fragrant with new-mown hay, and that judicious David, and a tender sweetness in Christabel's blue eyes, had been too much for him, and the words had come of their own accord somehow, he hardly knew how.

Was he sorry when she looked up at him with those sweet eyes, brimming over with happy tears, and murmured shyly : —

" I thought you were going to marry Miss Perkington! "

" Not for millions of millions, darling! " he cried, not sorry, but rapturously glad, clasping the slender figure to his breast, and raining down kisses on the fair young face.

David drew nearer at this juncture, still intent upon astronomical study, but with the air of thinking he might be wanted presently.

Frank took the hint, released the trembling girl, quite confounded by surprise and joy, and put a little hand through his arm with the calmest air of appropriation.

" It's all settled, darling," he said; " I shall call upon your father to-morrow."

" O Mr. Greenwood! "

" Mr. Greenwood! If you say that again, I shall kiss you again, in spite of David."

" Frank, then."

How sweet it was to say it! how sweet it was to hear it! — sweetness known to youth only, that loves and is beloved for the first time. After six or seven such experiences, that sort of thing is apt to become commonplace. It is like one's first watch, one's first Derby day, one's first whitebait dinner.

" I'm sure your father will never let you marry me, Frank," said Christabel.

" I should like to see myself asking my governor's permission," replied the young man. " He ought to be proud of my getting such a chance — marrying a girl of a grand, old family like yours; Brummagem allying itself to the Middle Ages; counting-house getting a leaf in Burke's ' County Families.' "

"But we are so poor," remonstrated Christabel. "At least—"

"A lift in the social scale is better than money, my dearest. I can take out letters-patent and call myself Greenwood-Champion by and by. That would look well upon our pasteboards, wouldn't it, Belle?"

They were in the deep shadow of the trees by this time. Not a glimmer of light was visible in the old house. All the lower windows were closely guarded by heavy oak shutters. They went to a little door—not the principal entrance, but a low, arched door in a side tower—and David rang a bell, which made a tremendous clanging half a mile away, as it seemed. They had to wait a considerable time before any one answered this summons, very much to Frank's satisfaction. He was whispering schemes about their future life into Christabel's ear, just as if they had been engaged a twelvemonth; while David looked up at the dark ivy-covered walls, as if calculating the sparrows' nests.

Some one came at last—much too soon for Francis Greenwood. Slipshod feet shuffled along a stone passage, uncertain hands fumbled with locks and bolts, and the door being opened cautiously, revealed the ancient butler in a semi-somnambulistic condition.

"Lard, but you be late, Miss Chrissy," he said; he had helped to nurse her in her motherless babyhood. "Your pa's gone to bed ever so long."

"I'm glad of that," Christabel whispered to her lover.

"Why, sweetest?"

"Because I never *could* have told him; and if he had seen my face, he might have found out—"

"He shall hear all about it to-morrow, darling. I shall call at one o'clock."

"And I shall ride Gilpin away to the other end of the world. I couldn't bear to be in the house while—while—"

"While I am in the dock," said the young man, laughing. "I think the verdict will be a favorable one, Chrissy."

"Oh, you don't know," cried Christabel, dolefully.

"I don't know what, dear?"

"How prejudiced papa is against your family, because of the new Hall being built upon land that once belonged to this, and the estate having been cut up and spoiled so, to make your grounds. Those meadows of yours were a part of our park once."

"That isn't our fault, darling, but that improvident old Champion's. Who knows but what the two estates might be joined somehow one of these days? My father could buy himself another place; and we'd cut off the new Hall with the smallest possible allowance of garden, and restore this dear old barn " — so lightly did young Oxford speak of a perfect specimen of Tudor architecture — "to its original splendor."

The sleepy butler coughed faintly, as if to remind them of his infirmities and the lateness of the hour. It was nearly midnight by this time — that walk across the fields had lasted so long. The lovers clasped hands, and said good-night; and Frank would fain have made this last good-night a long business, only there was the butler, with his guttering tallow candle and his piteous, expostulating look, and David in the rear yawning audibly. So with one warm pressure of the little hand he let her go, and the stout old door closed upon her, like the jaws of a monster that had just swallowed her up.

Francis Greenwood turned away with a sigh, putting his hand in his waistcoat-pocket mechanically to give · David baksheesh. But David had vanished, and the court-yard was empty. He looked about him meditatively, in no humor to go back to the common world just yet. The wind was sighing faintly among the ivy-leaves, with a sound scarce louder than the breathing of a quiet sleeper; the black wall of the old house rose high above him, the shadow of it fell upon him like a pall.

"What a dismal place for my pet to live in!" he said to himself, and then began to wonder which was her room, and to watch for the glimmer of a light from one of those upper casements.

It came presently; a feeble twinkle, which flitted along a corridor, shining faintly from a row of narrow windows, and then stopped and grew steady in a window at the end of the house. This was his darling's chamber, the young man thought rapturously. It might have been the butler's, but fortunately was not; that functionary — who might have had his pick of twenty vacant rooms — preferring to inhabit a darksome den in the steep, sloping roof, where he burrowed like a rabbit. It really was Christabel's room.

Rudderford church clock struck twelve while the lover still stood gazing, and at that very moment, as if conjured into being by the last stroke of the mystic hour, the figure of a man came suddenly from behind an angle of the wall.

"Who the deuce are you?" cried Frank, darting forward.

But the figure had vanished. There was a labyrinth of outbuildings on that side of the house. Frank followed, and prowled round about them, peering into every corner, but could find no trace of that midnight intruder. There is always a nook into which that sort of gentry can screw itself. His search was so close and thorough, that he began at last to fancy his own senses must have deceived him, and that the figure had been only a creature of the imagination. He was not easily satisfied, however. The jewel in that old Tudor casket was to his mind so rare a gem, that no care or watchfulness could be too much for him, whose privilege it was to guard it. He made a complete circuit of the house, trying windows and shutters. On the lower story all was secure as the casements of a beleaguered fortress, close guarded from the foe. If Anthony Champion had been the owner of hoarded millions, he could scarcely have protected himself better from possible burglars.

One o'clock struck before Frank Greenwood left the precincts of the old Hall, and walked slowly away towards the meadows.

CHAPTER V.

CHRISTABEL was almost too happy after that midnight parting. There was no depressing influence tonight in the gloom and silence of her ancient home. All the burden of her loneliness, which she had borne so meekly, was lifted away in a moment, and her future life lay radiant before her, like a garden in fairy-land. She was a little anxious about her father, and his strong prejudices against the race of Greenwood; but her lover appeared to her altogether so fascinating and irresistible, that she could not imagine anybody proof against his influence. Her father would like and admire him, of course, just as she did, and would abandon all his prejudices, and accept him as her lover. And Miss Perkington! Christabel laughed aloud — a little, happy laugh that startled the silence of the old room — at the thought of that young lady's ignominious defeat: all the silk flounces and lace frillings counting for nothing in the eyes of true love.

She was much too happy to think of sleep for ever so long, although it was past midnight, but paced the room, with her hands clasped in a joyous reverie, thinking of the wondrous fortune that had befallen her. Only a retired manufacturer's son, it is true; but then she loved him, and he seemed to her the one most perfect creature in all the world — so bright, so generous, so brave, so true. She had known so few people, had lived

132

a life so utterly lonely, that it is scarcely strange she should believe in the one sunny-natured young fellow who had praised
and loved her.

Here she stopped before the tall narrow old glass, and looked
at herself half wonderingly.

Was she really pretty? was she worthy of such a lover? She
shook out her long loose hair. Yes; she was like a picture of
Patient Grisel she remembered seeing years ago in a famous
collection.

The clock struck one before she lay down; and then, over-
come suddenly by sleep in the midst of her happy thoughts,
she threw herself down, dressed as she was, upon a sofa, to rest
a little before going seriously to bed; and thereupon fell into a
deep slumber, which seemed likely to last all night.

She had one bad habit, engendered perhaps of lonely days,
with much time for thoughtfulness and waking dreams — the
habit of walking in her sleep. It was not a thing that happened
to her often, but once in a way; two or three times in a year
perhaps, when her mind had been in any way disturbed during
the day, she had been wont to wonder. The servants had met
her at daybreak, sometimes in the corridor, or out on the broad
square landing beyond, or on the stairs even, descending ghost-
like, with open, unseeing eyes. One luckless country lass, taking
her for a ghost of that slaughtered lady whose spirit was reported to haunt the Hall, had fled shrieking to the kitchen,
where she fell into violent hysterics, clutching the air, and wellnigh strangling herself with her sobs and screams.

And so it happened to-night. Towards three o'clock, just as
the moon was waning, the girl rose from her sofa, pushed open
the door, which she had left ajar, and went out into the corridor
— a tall white figure faintly visible in the dim light.

She went straight on to an angle of the corridor where there
was a narrow window cut in a part of the wall where the ivy

grew thickest. As she came slowly forward, this window was opened by a stealthy hand, and a man thrust his head and shoulders through the window.

He was on the point of leaping through, when his eyes — evil eyes they were, too — fell upon that mysterious figure, with the white dress and loose flowing hair, the figure he had heard of many a time, when folks talked of the ghost that haunted Old Rudderford Hall.

He dropped his stick with an ejaculation. The fall of the jagged stake, cut from a hedge, and trimmed with a rough, hasty hand, upon the uncarpeted oak floor awakened Christabel. She gave a loud shriek, and stared at the intruder transfixed. That shriek was alarming enough; but it reassured him. He sprang into the corridor, and clapped his great horny hand upon her mouth.

"What, it's you, is it?" he exclaimed, in a cautious voice. "Hold your row; or I shall have to quiet you with my clasp-knife. What brings you prowling about at this time of night, I wonder? After that chap that was prowling outside an hour ago, I suppose. Come, young lady, you just walk into your own room, and keep yourself to yourself; I've got business to do here."

He had tied a big bird's-eye handkerchief across the girl's mouth — she was not fully awake yet, and had only a confused sense of peril and horror — and had just produced another, with a view to tying it round her wrists, when a great crash of glass sounded close behind him, and Frank Greenwood sprang through the open window, smashing the casement as he came through.

Love is so foolish, so full of morbid doubts and apprehensions. He had come back to the old Hall, after crossing the meadows on his way home, not able to feel comfortable about that lurking figure which he had seen at midnight, and had come back just in time to rescue his betrothed from the clutch of a ruffian, and to save the Champion diamonds, — a very valuable portion of his future wife's dowry.

The man was Black Simeon the poacher. He had been lurking about the night before, when Mr. Champion showed his daughter the family jewels, had seen the gems and where they were kept, and had hidden himself in the shrubbery when Christabel came out to reconnoitre. To-night he had tried all the lower doors and windows, and finding entrance below impossible, had clambered up the ivy to this casement at the end of the corridor, trusting to his good luck to grope his way downstairs to the library.

The intent but not the deed confounded him. He was pinioned and locked in an empty wine-cellar that night, and handed over to the local authorities at breakfast-time, to appear by and by, charged with a burglarious attempt, and to return to that state of bondage from which he had so lately emerged.

Anthony Champion could hardly be uncivil to the man who had saved his daughter and the family diamonds; and Frank Greenwood really was a nice young fellow, with free-and-easy, irresistible ways. He brought brightness and life into the gloomy old house, and in an incredibly short time persuaded the master of Old Rudderford Hall to waive his prejudices against the inmates of New Rudderford Hall.

When he had smoothed the way by his artful management, he coolly ordered his father to call upon Mr. Champion, to entreat that gentleman's consent to the union of the two houses. The manufacturer was furious, and there was a scene; but a very brief one. Frank's supreme coolness made light of everything. Miss Perkington had departed before this in silent disgust, with all her baggage. Samuel Greenwood was fain to give way; it evidently mattered so very little to his son whether he did or not.

" I can always make a living at the bar," said young Oxford in his careless way, " and there's the five hundred a year my poor mother left me. I should like to have made an amicable arrangement, and secured your co-operation for restoring the old Hall; but if it isn't to be, why it isn't; you know best; and we shan't starve."

Samuel fretted and fumed, swore an oath or two, and succumbed. He went to call upon Mr. Champion with lamb-like meekness, and returned crestfallen.

Mr. Champion was prepared to waive all consideration of the wide difference between the status of the two families, and to consent to the marriage. He could give his daughter fifty thousand pounds, and jewels worth at least twenty-five thousand more. Mr. Greenwood had supposed him to be a pauper.

" It has been my fancy to live like this," he said, " and allow the surplus of my income to accumulate for my only child."

And so they were married, and were just the sort of couple to live happily ever afterwards.

THE MOUNTAIN CHILD.

THE MOUNTAIN CHILD.

BY WILLIAM WORDSWORTH.

MONG the hills of Athol he was born,
Where, on a small hereditary farm,
An unproductive slip of rugged ground,
His parents, with their numerous offspring, dwelt,
A virtuous household, though exceeding poor!
Pure livers were they all, austere and grave,
And fearing God; the very children taught
Stern self-respect, a reverence for God's Word,
And an habitual piety, maintained
With strictness scarcely known on English ground.

From his sixth year, the boy of whom I speak,
In Summer tended cattle on the hills;
But, through the inclement and the perilous days
Of long-continuing Winter he repaired,
Equipped with satchel, to a school, that stood
Sole building on a mountain's dreary edge,
Remote from view of city spire, or sound
Of minster clock. From that bleak tenement,
He, many an evening, to his distant home
In solitude returning, saw the hills
Grow larger in the darkness, all alone
Beheld the stars come out above his head,
And travelled through the wood with no one near
To whom he might confess the things he saw.
So the foundations of his mind were laid.
In such communion, not from terror free,
While yet a child, and long before his time,
He had perceived the presence and the power
Of greatness; and deep feelings had impressed
Great objects on his mind, with portraiture
And color so distinct, that on his mind

THE MOUNTAIN CHILD.

They lay like substances, and almost seemed
To haunt the bodily sense. He had received
A precious gift; for, as he grew in years,
With these impressions would he still compare
All his remembrances, thoughts, shapes, and forms;
And, being still unsatisfied with aught
Of dimmer character, he thence attained
An active power to fasten images
Upon his brain; and on their pictured lines
Intensely brooded, even till they acquired
The liveliness of dreams. Nor did he fail,
While yet a child, with a child's eagerness
Incessantly to turn his ear and eye
On all things which the moving seasons brought
To feed such appetite : nor this alone
Appeased his yearning : — in the after-day
Of boyhood, many an hour in caves forlorn
And 'mid the hollow depths of naked crags,
He sate, and even in their fixèd lineaments,
Or from the power of a peculiar eye,
Or by creative feeling overborne,
Or by predominance of thought oppressed,
Even in their fixed and steady lineaments
He traced an ebbing and a flowing mind,
Expressions ever varying.

THE
GLEANERS AT THE STILE.

THE GLEANERS AT THE STILE.

BY TOM TAYLOR.

BY paths that ran through spikèd sheaves,
  Or stubbles russet green,
Girt with their belt of living leaves,
  I strolled to sketch the scene.

Gold framed in emerald! hedge-row bound,
  New-reaped or wheat-clad square,
And purple fallow, to the round
  Of woodland-distance fair.

Foot-ways that wound through corn-flowers blue,
  Red poppies, nodding wheat,
To brakes, where, light in shadow, grew
  The stately meadow-sweet.

A group of gleaners came in sight,
  Resting about a stile;
Unseen, I marked their dark and light,
  They talking free the while.

Their talk ran on their harvest-spoil,
  The bushels gleaned and shelled;
Each boasting how her childish toil
  The household store had swelled.

The meadow-sweet breathed fragrantly,
  The elms swung overhead,
But what of beauty spoke to me,
  To them spoke, first, of bread.

Thenceforth the sweetness of the scene,
  Methought, more solemn grew,
With threads of human toil and teen
  Enwoven through and through.

RECOLLECTIONS OF
OLE BULL.

RECOLLECTIONS OF OLE BULL.

BY L. MARIA CHILD.

UL, in the language of Norway, means the trunk of a tree, and doubtless has the same origin as the Saxon word Bole, so often used by Dryden, and the older English poets. The musical Christian name is extremely common in Norway. Two friends seeing a boat full of fishermen about to land, one of them laid a wager that more than half of them were named Ole. Upon inquiry, it was found they *all* bore that name, except one, and he was called Ole Olesson, or Ole the son of Ole. At home, the popular title of the beloved and honored musician is "Ole Olesson Fiole," or Ole the Violin.

This allusion to the violin calls to mind one among many envious remarks which have been excited by his extraordinary popularity. It has been said that he does not, like a true artist, rely on his own genius for success, but resorts to tricks to excite and interest the public, such as romantic fictions about his violin, &c. Those who know his unpretending simplicity and manly independence of character are well aware that the charge is most unjust. The romantic history of his violin is no fiction, and few men could possess such a unique gem and say so little about it as he does. He sometimes tells its history to friends, in answer to inquiries

147

which the singularity of its appearance naturally excites; and if *they* impart the information to the public, it is merely what they would very naturally do concerning anything so curious in the history of art.

This remarkable instrument was manufactured by Gaspar da Salo, in Brescia, one of the three oldest violin makers on record; and it was considered the best one he ever made. It was sculptured at Rome by the famous Benvenuto Cellini, celebrated as a goldsmith in his early life, and afterward as a sculptor. Pope Clement VII. employed him to make a variety of medals, golden chalices, and other rich ornaments for churches and palaces. One of them, a present from the Pope to Charles V., was a beautifully illuminated prayer-book, which cost the Cardinal de Medici above two thousand crowns. The golden covers were wrought by Cellini with figures in basso-relievo, and enamelled arabesques, studded with rich jewels. The Emperor was exceedingly struck with the beauty of the design and workmanship, in which he at once recognized the hand of an extraordinary artist. Indeed, so decidedly did everything he touched bear the impress of genius, that stamps which he made for coins in the Roman mint are still preserved as rare specimens of art. Michael Angelo and Titian were his friends, and thought very highly of his productions. He was a great favorite with Francis I., for whom he executed many admirable works in gold, silver and bronze. Though accustomed for years to make small figures with exquisite delicacy of finish, he produced, later in life, several noble works on a grander scale. The most celebrated of these is a statue of Perseus in bronze, executed for Duke Cosmo, of Florence.

The violin now in possession of Ole Bull was made to the order of Cardinal Aldobrandini, one of a noble family at Rome, memorable for their patronage of the fine arts. He gave for it 3000 Neapolitan ducats, and presented it to the treasury of Innspruck, where it became a celebrated curiosity, under the name of "The Treasury Chamber Violin." When that city was taken by the French in 1809, it was carried to Vienna and sold to Rjheazhek, a wealthy Bohemian, whose splendid collection of rare and ancient stringed instruments had attracted universal attention in the musical world. The gem of his museum was the violin manufactured by Da Salo and sculptured by Cellini. He was offered immense sums for it by English, Russian and Polish noblemen; but to all such offers he answered by demanding the price of half Vienna.

A few years ago Ole Bull gave fifteen concerts in Vienna, with the brilliant success which usually attends him. The Bohemian, who went with the crowd to hear him, was an enthusiastic admirer of his genius, and soon became personally acquainted with him. Until then he had considered himself the most learned man in Europe in the history of violins, the peculiar merits of all the most approved manufacturers, and the best methods of repairing deficiencies, or improving the tones. But with Ole Bull, love of the violin had been an absorbing passion from his earliest childhood. He never saw one of a novel shape, or heard one with a new tone, without studying into the causes of the tone and the effects produced by the shape. Through every nook and corner of Italy he sought for new varieties of his favorite instrument as eagerly as an Oriental merchant seeks for rare pearls. He had tried all manner of experiments; he knew at sight the tuneful qualities of every species of wood, and precisely how the slightest angle or curve in the fashion of an instrument would affect the sound. He imparted to the Bohemian amateur much information that was new and valuable; and this sympathy of tastes and pursuits produced a warm friendship between them. Of course, Ole looked with a longing eye on the oldest and best of his violins; but the musical antiquarian loved it like an only child. He could not bring himself to sell it at that time, but he promised that if he ever did part with it, the Minstrel of Norway should have the preference over every other man in the world. He died two years afterward, and a letter from his son informed Ole Bull that his dying father remembered the promise he had given. He purchased it forthwith, and it was sent to him at Leipsic.

On the head of this curious violin is carved and colored an angel's face, surrounded by flowing curls of hair. Behind this figure, leaning against the shoulders, is a very beautiful little mermaid, the human form of which terminates in scales of green and gold. The neck of the instrument is ornamented with arabesques in blue, red and gold. Below the bridge is a mermaid in bronze. Thorwaldsen took great delight in examining these figures, and bestowed enthusiastic praise on the gracefulness of the design and the excellence of the workmanship. Ole Bull was born in February, and by an odd coincidence the bridge of his darling violin is delicately carved with two intertwined fishes, like the zodiacal sign of February. Two little tritons, cut in ivory, are in one corner of the bow. Altogether, it is a very original and singularly beautiful instrument. It has the rich look of the middle ages, and would have been a right royal gift for some princely troubadour. Amateurs praise its fine proportions, and say that its form combines many of the characteristics of Amati, Stradivarius and Guarnerius. Indeed, it is universally admitted to be the most valuable violin in the world. The wood is extremely soft and very thick. The upper covering is of an exceedingly rare species of Swiss pine, celebrated in the manufacture of violins. It grows on the Italian side of the Alps, for sunshine and song seem inseparably connected, and the balmy atmosphere which makes Italy so rich in music, and imparts to her language such liquid melody, seems breathed into her trees.

Those acquainted with music are well aware that the value of an instrument is prodigiously increased by the age of the wood, and that the purity of its tone depends very much on the skilfulness of the hand which has played upon it. As the best and brightest human soul can never free itself entirely from the influence of base and vulgar associations in youth, so a violin never quite recovers from the effect of discordant vibrations. So perceptible is this to a delicate ear, that when Ole Bull first performed in Philadelphia he at once perceived that the double bass viol in the orchestra was a very old instrument, and had been well played on. Some time after, the horse and rider that represented General Putnam's leap down the precipice, plunged into the orchestra of the theatre, and crushed the old bass viol. As soon as Ole Bull became aware of the accident, he hastened to buy the fragments. The wood of his violin was so old, and so thoroughly vibrated, that he had never been able to obtain a sounding post adapted to it. This post is an extremely small piece of wood in the interior of the instrument, but the inharmonious vibration between the old and the new disturbed his sensitive ear until he was enabled to remedy the slight defect by a fragment of the double bass.

One of the most curious facts in connection with this memorable violin is, that it was probably never played upon by any other hand than Ole Bull's, though it is three hundred years old. It had always been preserved as a curiosity, and when it came into his possession it had no bar inside, nor any indication that such a necessary appendage had ever been put into it. The inward spiritual carving has been entirely done by this "Amphion of the North," as he is styled by Andersen, the celebrated Danish novelist. The interior is completely covered with indentations in ovals and circles, produced by the vibration of his magic tones. Doubtless the angels could sing from them fragmentary melodies of the universe; but to us they reveal no more than wave-marks on the shores of the ever-rolling sea.

Whatever importance may be attached to one or other of the circumstances connected with the history of this violin, all America can testify to the peculiar sweetness and purity of its tone; nor can the combined musical criticism of the world ever convince Americans that it was not the genuine power of genius which carried this heavenly voice so deep into the universal heart of the nation. They can never be reasoned out of the feeling that the most skilful artistic performances, compared with those simple but richly tinted melodies, are like the cold beauty of a statue in contrast with the bright, warm coloring of Titian.

The story that Paganini bequeathed one of his violins to Ole Bull is a fiction. He never owned an instrument that had belonged to the renowned Italian. The other violin, which he brought to the United States with him, is a Cremona, made in 1742 by the famous manufacturer, Joseph Guarnerius. The diamonds in the bow, forty-five in number, were presented to Ole Bull by the Queen of Norway and Sweden.

One day, when he returned to his lodgings in Paris, he found his two little boys dragging these two precious violins about the floor. They had tied strings to them, and thought they made extremely pretty carts. The eldest, being a very sensitive child, turned pale when his father entered with an exclamation of surprise and distress. His terrified look touched the tender-hearted parent, and he began to caress the children instead of scolding them, for he reflected that the poor little souls could not know the profanation of which they had been guilty in dragging about a Da Salo and a Guarnerius for playthings.

Ole Bull owns several violins. One of them is a Cremona, made in 1687, for the king of Spain, by Antonius Stradivarius. The wood is very flexible, and it is elaborately finished, being inlaid with garlands of ebony and ivory, intertwisted with serpents and little birds. He never speaks of it without dwelling with delighted enthusiasm on its "sweet, insinuating voice." To hear him talk of his violins, one would suppose he was describing a band of beloved human beings, or a collection of rare singing birds at the least. No other instrument has ever inspired musicians with such enthusiastic and absorbing affection, for no other gives such full utterance to the yearnings of the heart.

His passion for violins manifested itself at a very early age. A maternal uncle, who was passionately fond of music, frequently had quartette clubs at his house. He played well on the violoncello, and had a curious collection of rare instruments. He loved to amuse himself with little Ole's extreme susceptibility to music. When he was three years old he often put him in the violoncello case, and hired him with sweetmeats to stay there while he played. But the candy could not keep him quiet long. The eyes gradually kindled, and the little feet began to beat time. At last his nervous excitement would become too great to admit of his staying in the violoncello case. The music was dancing all through him, and he must give it utterance. When he returned home he would seize the yard measure, and, with a small stick for a bow, endeavor to imitate what his uncle had played. He heard it with the inward ear all the time; but for fear his parents were not so pervaded with the tune as he was, he would explain as he went along, telling how beautifully the bass came in at such and such a place. At five years old his uncle bought him a very small violin, as yellow as a lemon. He says he never felt carried up into the third heaven as he did when his own little hand first brought out a tune from that yellow violin. He loved it and kissed it; it seemed to him so beautiful, that little yellow violin! To the surprise of the family, he immediately played well upon it, though he had received no instruction. He had always been present at the family concerts, and he observed everything and remembered everything. On his little yellow violin he played a quartette of Pleyel's to the assembled club, and they inquired with astonishment who had taught the child, for they knew not that God had taught him by a process as simple as that of the mocking-bird.

When he was eight years old, a Frenchman arrived in Bergen with violins for sale. One of them, bright red in its color, gained the boy's heart at first sight, and he pleaded with his father till he consented to buy it. It was purchased late in the afternoon and put away in its case. Ole slept in a small bed in the same apartment with his parents, and the much-coveted instrument was in the adjoining room. "I could not sleep," said he, "for thinking of my new violin. When I heard father and mother breathing deep, I rose softly and lighted a candle, and in my night-clothes did go on tiptoe to open the case and take one little peep. The violin was so red, and the pretty pearl screws did smile at me so! I pinched the strings just a little with my fingers. It smiled at me ever more and more. I took up the bow and looked at it. It said to me that it would be pleasant to try it across the strings. So I did try it, just a very, very little; and it did sing to me so sweetly! Then I did creep further away from the bedroom. At first I did play very soft. I make very, very little noise. But presently I did begin a capriccio, which I like very much; and it did go ever louder and louder; and

I forgot that it was midnight, and that everybody was asleep. Presently I hear something go crack! and the next minute I feel my father's whip across my shoulders. My little red violin dropped on the floor and was broken. I weep much for it, but it did no good. They did have a doctor to it next day, but it never recovered its health."

Ole Bull never learned to read music by the usual method. From infancy he had been accustomed to hear music frequently, and he knew the sound of each written note long before he could call it by name. At ten years old, a foreign music master urged upon his father the necessity of having him taught scientifically. The attempt was accordingly made. He was instructed how to hold his violin and handle his bow according to rule, and was told that he must leave off improvising, and practise by note. He could at that time play a capriccio of Paganini's, considered impracticable by older and skilful performers; but nothing would come to him by the mechanical process. His genius positively refused to go into the strait-jacket; and when father and teacher coaxed and scolded, the nervous child at last screamed with agony. This untamable freedom was his earliest characteristic, and will probably remain strongest to the last. At school, the confinement of four walls would sometimes press upon him so that he would suddenly spring out of the window into God's sunshine and free air. He would leap fences, swim rivers, scale precipices, turn somersets on horses, and climb to the tops of high trees to rock himself in the wind. The manner in which he dived and rushed about caused the family to bestow on him the name of "The Bat."

It is this abhorrence of fetters which now imparts to his genius that freshness and overleaping life which constitutes its greatest charm. Critics constantly complain that he pays no attention to the rules; but the public everywhere agree that they do not care for this, so long as the glow of his music warms and electrifies their souls.

The Concerto in E Minor, played at his farewell concert in this city, is a favorite composition with him, but he seldom brings it out, on account of the difficulty of the instrumentation. It was composed at Prague, for the benefit of the widows and orphans of musicians. He imagined a daughter lingering by the bed-side of her departed father, with whom she had watched during the night. The intensity of grief gradually becomes calmer, and is mingled with pleasant recollections of childhood, as the faint gleams of morning dispel the darkness of night. To express this flickering twilight, the different parts of the orchestra play in different rhythm. One is in four-time, and the other in six-eight, while his violin alternates between the two. Light triumphs, the uncertainty vanishes, and with the bright aurora all comes into the same rhythm. "This contrariety of rhythm in the different parts is one of the things in which they accuse me of violating the rules," said he; "but what do I care? It produces the effect I wish to produce; and I have always regarded many of the rules of music as perfectly arbitrary and useless." This Concerto in E Minor is extremely beautiful and poetic. In the part which expresses deep grief, the music sobs audibly, and the adagio movement of twilight is indescribably sweet and dreamy.

"The Mother's Prayer," which has been such a universal favorite in this country, was composed at Florence, at the request of the Dominicans, who wanted some new music for their church. He promised to do it, but neglected it from day to day. At last, they waited upon him early in the morning, and told him it *must* be ready for rehearsal the next day. "I was in bed when they came," said he; "I had been up all night with the moon, sympathizing with her. I had thought of Norway, of home, and of many sad things. I said to the Dominicans that they should have their music the next morning. So I took my violin, and it did sing to me so sweetly the thoughts of the night! It spoke to me so kindly! I wrote down its voice, and the Dominicans complained it was too plaintive. They said they already had so much sad, solemn music, that they wanted something cheerful. So I did compose something in a more lively strain for them; and because this brought before me the image of a mother kneeling at the altar, entreating for her child, I called it 'The Mother's Prayer.'" These friars became very warmly attached to him, and tried hard to persuade him to join their fraternity. A tame finale this would have been, to the life-opera, which began with swinging to the winds in the tops of Norwegian pines.

The "Polacca Guerriera" was first conceived at Naples, alone at midnight, gazing on Mt. Vesuvius, flaming through the darkness. He went to Rome soon after, and carried the vague conception in his mind, intending to arrange it there, and bring it out at his first concert. At Rome he shared the apartment of a talented young artist, who became warmly attached to him. The intimate relation between music and painting was a favorite theme with this young man, and to the musician the sounds of an orchestra had always suggested colors. When he slept late in the morning, the artist would often rouse him, by saying, "Come, Ole, get up and play to me! I can't paint unless you play to me." Being urged and urged, he would at last shake off his drowsiness, and, half-dressed, begin to play. The violin would soon absorb him, till an exclamation from the painter broke in upon his reverie. "Ah, dear Ole, give me that once more. It is such a brilliant red!" or, "Play that again, dear Ole, it is such a heavenly blue."

Thorwaldsen, who was then at Rome, loved Ole Bull with most devoted affection, and delighted in his genius. These friends, of course, felt a deep interest in his success. From day to day they would ask whether he had done anything toward completing the Polacca. His answer always was, "No, but I *shall* do it." As the time for the concert drew nigh, they remonstrated against such dangerous delay. "How can you be so careless of your fame, Ole?" said Thorwaldsen. "Do try to have this new piece done in season; if not for your own sake, at least for mine; for, independent of my affection for you, you know I claim you as a countryman, and my pride of country is at stake." * The concert was advertised, and the Polacca was in the programme; still, it had no existence, except in the musician's soul. "*Have* you written that music?" said Thorwaldsen. "*Are* you crazy?" inquired the painter. But he would throw his arms around them, and laugh and jest, as if his musical reputation concerned everybody more than it did himself. The day before the concert his friends were in despair when they saw him prepare to go out after breakfast. "Have you written any of that music?" said they, entreatingly. "No, my dear friends, but I have it all here," replied he, playfully touching his forehead. They urged that the concert was to be the next day, and that the piece must be rehearsed. "I will do it this evening," said he. "You are an imprudent man," they replied; "the public of Rome will not bear such treatment. You will make a complete failure." He laughed, and coaxed them caressingly not to be troubled on his account. The evening was far spent when he returned. The artist, in anxious tones, asked, "Dear Ole, *have* you done anything about that music?" "No, I have not had time." "Well, do set about it this moment."

---

* Norway and Denmark are included under the same government.

"Oh, I cannot; I am so tired that I must go directly to bed."
In vain the artist remonstrated and entreated. A spirit of
mischief had taken possession of the wayward minstrel. He
plunged into bed, and soon pretended to be sound asleep.
The young man had the habit of talking to himself, and as
he listened to the bass solo of the counterfeit sleeper, he muttered, "How *can* he go to sleep with nothing done about that
music? It is more than I can comprehend. I wish I could
feel as easy about it as he does." He retired to rest early,
and as soon as he was fairly asleep Ole sprang out of bed,
lighted a candle, and stepped softly into an adjoining room,
where he began to write down his music with prestissimo
speed. The outline had long been in his mind, and new
thoughts for the filling up came with a rush of inspiration.
He wrote as fast as the pen could fly. At four o'clock the
score for all the orchestral parts was written out. For his
violin part he trusted entirely to his own wonderful memory.
Having arranged all, he crept quietly back into his bed. The
artist, who was an early riser, soon began to stir. Ole breathed
sonorously, as if he were in a deep sleep. "Still asleep,"
murmured his friend, "as quietly as if the music were all
ready for the orchestra. I wish we were safely through this
evening." It was not long before his anxiety took a more
active form. He began to shake the sleeper, saying, "Ole,
do wake up, and try to do something about the music." But
he obtained only the drowsy answer, "Oh, I cannot, I am so
very sleepy." Vexed and discouraged, the painter went to
his easel and said no more. At breakfast Ole was full of fun
and frolic; but Thorwaldsen and the artist were somewhat
impatient with what they deemed such thoughtless trifling
with public expectation. "You will come to my concert to-
night, will you not?" said the mischievous musician. In dismal tones they replied : "No, Ole; we love you too well to

witness your disgrace. Take it as lightly as you please; but you may be assured the public of Rome will not bear such treatment." "Oh, do come," pleaded the musician, coaxingly. Just a little, *little* within the door; and then, when I am disgraced, you can easily slip away." They would not promise, however, and he hurried off to keep his appointment with the orchestra. He had an excellent band of musicians who could play the most difficult music with the slightest preparation. The rehearsal went off to his complete satisfaction, and he returned to his friends as gay as a lark. His apparent recklessness made them still more sad. The dreaded evening came. The house was crowded. Ole was full of that joyful confidence which genius is so apt to feel in effusions that have just burst freshly from its overflowing fountain. The orchestra delighted in the composition, and played it with their hearts. The brilliancy of the theme and the uncommon beauty of the cantabile took the audience by surprise. The novelty and marvellous difficulty of the finale, in which the violin alone performs four distinct parts, and keeps up a continuous shake through fifteen bars, completely electrified them. There was a perfect tempest of applause. In the midst of his triumph, the composer, looking as quiet and demure as possible, glanced toward the door. There stood Thorwaldsen and the artist. The latter had a trick of moving tobacco from one side of his mouth to the other when he was excited and pleased. It was now flying from cheek to cheek almost as rapidly as the violin bow through the continuous shake of fifteen bars.

The moment he left the stage his friends rushed into his arms, exclaiming, "When on earth did you do it? Only tell us that. Oh, it was too beautiful!" "Don't be so gay, my dear friends," replied he, with mock gravity; "you know the public of Rome won't bear such trifling. Why did you come to witness my disgrace?"

The next day all Rome was ringing with praises of the Norwegian violinist. They knew not which to applaud most, his genius or his superhuman strength in performing the four distinct parts on the violin at once, and keeping up the motion of his bow with such lightning swiftness for so long a time. No person who has not tried it can conceive of the extreme difficulty of playing at once distinct parts on each of the strings. It requires muscles strong as iron, and elastic as india rubber. Paganini had sufficient elasticity, but not sufficient strength. Ole Bull is the only man in the world that ever did it. When the Parisians first heard him produce this wonderful effect of four violins, it seemed so incredible that a story was circulated in the papers that it was all a deception; that some other musician was playing two of the parts behind the scenes. Thus originated the charge of "charlatanry," so often and so unjustly repeated.

The Polacca brought its composer a brilliant reputation at once, and musical critics were obliged to content themselves with saying that it was not written in the right measure for a Polacca.

CORNFIELDS.

.

CORNFIELDS.

BY MARY HOWITT.

HEN on the breath of autumn breeze,
From pastures dry and brown,
Goes floating like an idle thought
The fair white thistle-down,
Oh, then what joy to walk at will
Upon the golden harvest hill!

What joy in dreamy ease to lie
Amid a field new shorn,
And see all round on sunlit slopes
The piled-up stacks of corn;
And send the fancy wandering o'er
All pleasant harvest-fields of yore.

I feel the day — I see the field,
The quivering of the leaves,
And good old Jacob and his house
Binding the yellow sheaves;
And at this very hour I seem
To be with Joseph in his dream.

I see the fields of Bethlehem,
And reapers many a one,
Bending under their sickles' stroke —
And Boaz looking on;
And Ruth, the Moabite so fair,
Among the gleaners stooping there.

CORNFIELDS.

Again I see a little child,
  His mother's sole delight, —
God's living gift of love unto
  The kind, good Shunamite;
To mortal pangs I see him yield,
And the lad bear him from the field.

The sun-bathed quiet of the hills,
  The fields of Galilee,
That eighteen hundred years ago
  Were full of corn, I see;
And the dear Saviour takes his way
Mid ripe ears on the Sabbath day.

Oh, golden fields of bending corn,
  How beautiful they seem!
The reaper-folk, the piled-up sheaves,
  To me are like a dream.
The sunshine and the very air
Seem of old time, and take me there.

LOOKING INTO THE WELL.

LOOKING INTO THE WELL.

BY LOUISE CHANDLER MOULTON.

I.

P in the maples the robins sung,
   The winds blew over the locusts high,
And along the path by their boughs o'erhung
   We wandered gaily — Lulu and I —
Wandered along in pleasant talk,
   Pausing our nursery tales to tell,
Till we came to the end of the shaded walk,
   And sat, at last, by the moss-grown well.
She was a child, and so was I:
   What matter, then, that we told our love —
Whispered it there, with no one nigh,
   Save birds that sang in the trees above.
I looked down into her shy blue eyes,
   She at my face in the shaded well;
I saw the glow to her fair cheek rise,
   Like red in the heart of an ocean shell.

II.

Again in the trees the robins sung —
   The gold had deepened upon her hair —
The locusts over the pathway hung,
   To look at her face so still and fair.
I said no word — I sat by her side,
   Contented to hold her hand in mine,
Dreaming of love and a fair young bride —
   Visions that truth had made divine.
The robin's song took a clearer tone,
   The sky was a tenderer, deeper blue;
Her face in the limpid waters shone,
   I thought her eyes were holy and true.

LOOKING INTO THE WELL.

III.

I walked alone to the shaded well,
    When locusts bloomed in the next year's June —
The shadows along my pathway fell,
    The wild birds sang a sorrowful tune.
She had given her shining hair's young gold,
    Her holy brow and her eyes of blue,
The form I had scarcely dared to fold,
    To a wealthy suitor who came to woo —
Sold, for jewels and land and name,
    Youth and beauty, and love and grace.
Alone I cursed the sin and shame,
    And started to see my own dark face
Mirrored there in the well below,
    With its haggard cheek and its lines of care,
Where I once had seen a girlish brow,
    And shy blue eyes and golden hair.

IV.

Years have passed since that summer day
    Went over the hills with its silent tread :
I walk alone where its glory lay —
    I am lonely, and Lulu is dead.
Dust is thick on her shining hair,
    A shroud is folded across her breast,
The winds blow over the locusts where
    She lies at last, alone and at rest.
Youth and beauty, and love and grace,
    Wealth and station, joy and pain ;
If she dream at all in that lonely place,
    She will know, at length, that her life was vain.

V.

I do not think of her heart's disgrace,
    Looking into the waters there,
For I seem to see once more a face
    With shy blue eyes and golden hair.
Out among men she walks by my side —
    For me she lives whom the world calls dead —
I talk at night to my shadow bride,
    And pillow in dreams her golden head.

They broke her heart — so the gossips tell —
  Who sold her hand for wealth and a name;
But I see her face in the cool, deep well,
  And its virginal beauty is still the same.

171

TREASURES OF THE DEEP.

TREASURES OF THE DEEP.

BY MRS. FELICIA HEMANS.

HAT hidest thou in thy treasure caves and cells,
Thou hollow-sounding and mysterious main?
Pale glistening pearls, and rainbow-colored shells,
Bright things which gleam unrecked of and in vain :
Keep, keep thy riches, melancholy sea !
We ask not such from thee.

Yet more, the depths have more ! What wealth untold,
Far down, and shining through their stillness, lies !
Thou hast the starry gems, the burning gold,
Won from ten thousand royal argosies. —
Sweep o'er thy spoils, thou wild and wrathful main !
Earth claims not these again.

Yet more, the depths have more ! Thy waves have rolled
Above the cities of a world gone by !
Sand hath filled up the palaces of old,
Sea-weed o'ergrown the halls of revelry. —
Dash o'er them, ocean ! in thy scornful play :
Man yields them to decay.

Yet more ! the billows and the depths have more !
High hearts and brave are gathered to thy breast !
They hear not now the booming waters roar,
The battle-thunder will not break their rest. —
Keep thy red gold and gems, thou stormy grave, —
Give back the true and brave !

Give back the lost and lovely ! those for whom
The place was kept at board and hearth so long,
The prayer went up through midnight's breathless gloom,
And the vain yearning woke 'midst festal song !
Hold fast thy buried isles, thy bowers o'erthrown —
But all is not thine own.

TREASURES OF THE DEEP.

To thee the love of woman hath gone down,
  Dark flow thy tides o'er manhood's noble head,
O'er youth's bright locks, and beauty's flowery crown :
  Yet must thou hear a voice — Restore the dead !
Earth shall reclaim her precious things from thee ! —
    Restore the dead, thou sea !

176

A SONG OF THE SNOW.

A Song of the Snow.

BY MARY B. DODGE.

I.

H, the falling of the flakes
  In these mute, weird days —
Oh, the flakes the north-wind shakes
  In its whirling, swirling ways --
Ye are but a preparation
  For the keenest life we know;
Hearts break out in jubilation
  At the coming of the snow!
And the sleds from out the cellar,
  And the cutter from the loft,
O'er which summer was a jailer,
  Now are jewelling the soft
Fleecy whiteness; and the laughter
  Of the children, and the bells
Shaken loose athwart the rafter,
  Each with merry promise swells.
Oh, the falling of the flakes,
  Falling, falling, softly falling—
  Oh, the earth in dreams a-calling
For more covering ere she wakes;
Oh, the pearls the snow is twining
  Round the trees' minutest stems,
Waiting, waiting for the shining
  Of the sun to fire the gems;
Oh, the music of the bells,
  Stirred to fitful palpitation,
And the hope that upward wells
  Through the snow's sweet liberation;
Oh, the falling of the flakes,
  Falling, falling, softly falling,
And the white, still joy it makes
        World-enthralling!

179

A SONG OF THE SNOW.

See! the passive joy, yet pregnant
Of the joy that shall be regnant
   When the sun calls out the bells;
Wakes the jingling, jocund jingling,
Wakes the free *roulade* of jingling
   Of the sleigh's impatient bells!

II.

Oh, the sun upon the snow
   In these clear, bright days —
And the glitter of the glow
   Wrought of gold and crystal rays —
Ye are yielding in fruition
   Rare, ripe clusters of the joy
That was but an intuition
   Yesterday, to girl and boy!
Now the sleds are coasting gaily
   Down the whitely mantled hill,
And no single shadow, grayly,
   In the crisp noon bodeth ill.
Scarlet capes and woollen mufflers
   Half the dainty darlings hide.
Whom the ruddy, roistering shufflers
   Promise soon to give a ride.
Oh, the chubby, wrapped-up Graces!
   Mark them, as at carnival,
Roguish life within their faces,
   Throwing balls about pell-mell!
And the skaters pirouetting
   On their skates of burnished steel!
And the fun when, sleds upsetting.
   Riders tumble " head o'er heel "!
Oh, the ringing of the voices,
   Shouting, screaming, res'nant ringing,
While the answering air rejoices
     Sharply stinging!
Hark! the noisy mirth yet pregnant
Of the joy that shall be regnant.
   When the moon calls out the bells;
Wakes the jingling. dulcet jingling,
Wakes the full *roulade* of jingling
   Of the sleigh's resilient bells!

III.

Oh, the moon's resplendent light
  In these pure, white days —
When above, below, the night
  Is with sheen of snow ablaze;
When the milky-way of angels
  To fresh stars has given birth,
And Love's luminous evangels
  Lie unfolded on the earth!
Oh, not strange such lucubration,
  Tempting love to read it right,
Proves a peerless invitation
  To the maiden and her knight!
And not strange that coursers airy,
  Shod with softly feathered shoon,
Bear the two to realms of faery,
  Where ring bells in wedding-tune;
Where the dreamland bells are chiming
  With the strings of bells so sweet —
Liquid bells that go a-rhyming
  To the coursers' dancing feet!
Oh, these all are nigh forgotten
  In the tingle and the flush
Of bewildering bliss begotten
  Of the first kiss and its blush!
Yet with fresher inspiration
  Fall the dancing, prancing feet,
While the bells in new libation
    Seem *more* sweet!
List! in chorus ever pregnant
Of a future joy more regnant,
  How the moon calls out the bells!
Wakes the jingling, tenderest jingling,
Wakes the soft *roulade* of jingling
  Of the sleigh's mellifluous bells!

IV.

Oh, the magic of the snow
  In these blithe, cold days
When both young and old o'erflow
  With a half-unconscious praise!

A SONG OF THE SNOW.

When the young heart's ready keys
  Stir unbidden with sweet numbers,
And the old heart's memories
  Break in rhythm from their slumbers!
Oh, the precious dews of heaven,
  Making fair the summer flowers,
Are not more divinely given
  Than the frost of winter hours.
Hither falls a stainless vision
  Till, above the billowy snow,
Bells ring out in blent allision
    To and fro;
Swelling drifts o'ertop the fences,
  Burying boundaries out of sight;
Infinite whiteness thrills the senses
    With delight!
Oh, the falling flakes are pregnant
Of a joy forever regnant
  When their charm inspires the bells :
Wakes the wild and mellow jingling,
Wakes the rich *roulade* of jingling
  Of the snow's entrancing bells!

GOING SOMEWHERE.

GOING SOMEWHERE.

A GENRE SKETCH BY THE DETROIT HUMORIST.

E had been to town-meeting, had once voyaged a hundred miles on a steamboat, and had a brother who had made the overland trip to California. She had been to quiltings, funerals, and a circus or two, and she knew a woman whose sister thought nothing of setting out on a railroad journey where she had to wait fifteen minutes at a junction and change cars at a depot.

So I found them — a cosy-looking old couple, sitting up very straight in their seats, and trying to act like old railroad travellers. A shadow of anxiety suddenly crossed her face; she became uneasy, and directly she asked : —

"Philetus, I act'lly b'leeve we've went and taken the wrong train ! "

"It can't be, nohow," he replied, seeming a little startled. "Didn't I ask the conductor, and didn't he say we was right?"

"Yaas, he did, but look out of the window and make sure. He might have been a-lyin' to us ! "

The old man looked out of the window at the flitting fences, the galloping telegraph poles, and the unfamiliar fields, as if

expecting to catch sight of some old landmark, and forgetting
for a moment that he was a thousand miles from home.

"I guess we're all right, Mary," he said, as he drew in his
head.

"Ask somebody — ask that man there!" she whispered.

"This is the train for Chicago, haint it?" inquired the old
man of the passenger in the next seat behind.

"This is the train," replied the man.

"There! didn't I say so?" chuckled the old gent.

"It may be — it may be!" she replied, dubiously; "but if
we are carried wrong it won't be my fault. *I* say that we are
wrong, and when we've been led to some pirate's cave and
butchered for our money ye'll wish you had heeded my words."

He looked out of the window again, opened his mouth as if
to make some inquiry of a boy sitting on the fence, and then
leaned back in his seat and sighed heavily. She shut her teeth
together as if saying that she could stand it if he could, and the
train sped along for several miles. He finally said: —

"Looks like rain over thar in the west. I hope the boys hev
got them oats in."

"That makes me think of that umbreller!" she exclaimed,
diving her hands among the parcels at their feet.

She hunted around for two or three minutes, growing red in
the face, and then straigthened up and hoarsely whispered: —

"*It's gone!*"

"W — what?" he gasped.

"That umbreller!"

"No!"

"Gone, hide and hair!" she went on; "that sky-blue umbreller which I have had ever since Marth died!"

He searched around, but it was not to be found.

"Waal, that's queer," he mused, as he straightened up.

"Queer! Not a bit. I've talked to ye and talked to ye, but

186

it does no good. Ye came from a heedless fam'ly, and ye'd forget to put on yer boots 'f I didn't tell ye to."

" None o' the Harrisons were ever in the poor-house! " he replied, in a cutting tone.

" Philetus — Philetus H. Harrison! " she continued, laying her hand on his arm, " don't ye dare twit me of that again! I've lived with ye nigh on to forty years, and waited on ye when ye had biles and the toothache and the colic, and when ye fell and broke yer leg; but don't push me to the wall! "

He looked out of the window, feeling that she had the advantage of him, and as she wiped her eyes, settled her glasses on her nose, and used up the next fifteen minutes in thinking of the past. Feeling thirsty, she reached down among the bundles, searched around, and her face was as pale as death as she straightened back and whispered : —

" *And that's gone, too!* "

" What now? " he asked.

" That bottle with the cold tea in it! "

" It's been stole! " he exclaimed, looking around the car as if expecting to see some one with the bottle to their lips.

" First the umbreller — then the bottle! " she gasped.

" I couldn't have left it, could I? "

" Don't ask me! That bottle has been in our family twenty years — ever since mother died, and now it's gone! Land only knows what I'll do for a camfire bottle when we git home — if we ever do."

" I'll buy one."

" Yes, I know ye are always ready to buy, and if it wasn't for me to restrain ye the money'd fly like feathers in the wind."

" Waal, I didn't have to mortgage my farm," he replied, giving her a knowing look.

" Twitting agin! 'It isn't enough that ye've lost a good umbreller and a camfire bottle, but ye must twit me o' this and that."

Her nose grew red, and tears came to her eyes, but as he was looking out of the window she said nothing further. Ten or fifteen minutes passed, and, growing restless, he called out to a man across the aisle: —

"What's the sile around here?"

"Philetus — Philetus H. Harrison! stop yer noise!" she whispered, poking him with her elbow.

"I just asked a question," he replied, resuming his old position.

"What'd yer brother Joab tell ye the last thing afore we left him?" she asked. "Didn't he say somebody'd swindle ye on the string game, the confidence game, or some other game? Didn't he warn ye agin rascals?"

"I haint seen no rascals."

"Of course ye hevn't, 'cause yer blind! *I* know that that man is a villun, and if they don't arrest him for murder afore we leave this train I'll miss my guess! *I* can read human natur' like a book."

There was another period of silence, broken by her saying: —

"I wish I knew that this was the train for Chicago."

"Course it is."

"How do you know?"

"'Cause it is."

"Wall, *I* know it aint, but if you are contented to rush along to destruction I shan't say a word. Only when yer throat is being cut don't call out that I didn't warn ye."

The peanut-boy came along, and the old man reached down for his wallet.

"Philetus, ye shan't squander that money after peanuts!" she exclaimed, using one hand to catch his arm and the other to wave the boy on.

" Didn't I earn it? "

" Yaas, you sold two cows to git money to go on this visit; but it's half gone now, and the land only knows how we'll get home! "

The boy passed on, and the flag of truce was hung out for another brief time. She recommenced hostilities by remarking : —

" I wish I hadn't cum."

He looked up, and then out of the window.

" I know what ye want to say ! " she hissed; " but it's a blessed good thing for ye that I did come ! If ye'd come alone ye'd have been robbed and murdered and gasped and scalped and sunk in the river afore now ! "

" Pooh ! "

" Yes, pooh 'f ye want to, but *I* know ! "

He leaned back, she settled herself anew, and by and by — He nodded.

She nodded.

And in sleep their gray heads touched, and his arm found its way along the back of the seat, and his hand rested on her shoulder.

It was only their way.

M. QUAD.

189

COWS IN THE POOL.

COWS IN THE POOL.

BY TOM TAYLOR.

IGHT I choose, with Æsop's bent,
Aptest type of self-content,
It should be a herd of cows.
Who when heat forbids to browse,
And when midges sting and tease,
In dry shadow of the trees,
Seek a still and sheltered pool,
Rush-begirt, and dark and cool,
And in knee-deep bath sedate,
Flick off flies and ruminate
On the fever and the fret
Of silly sheep whose hearts are set
On pasture in the sun's hot glare,
Or on the foolish flights in air
Of the swallows flashing by,
Now to stream and now to sky.
Do-nothing philosophers,
Whom nor midge stings, nor gad-fly stirs;
Who in serene contempt look down
On toilers in the world's fierce day,
Or on the flighty spirits frown,
That spend in fancy's flash and play
The hours you ruminate away
In tepid water and soft clay.

GOD'S WAITING.

GOD'S WAITING.

BY JEAN INGELOW.

RAND is the leisure of the earth;
She gives her happy myriads birth,
And after harvest fears not dearth,
  But goes to sleep in snow-wreaths dim:
Dread is the leisure up above,
The while He sits whose name is Love,
And waits, as Noah did the dove,
  To see if she would fly to him.
He waits for us while, houseless things,
We beat about with bruised wings
On the dark floods and water-springs,
  The ruined world, the desolated sea;
With open windows from the prime,
All night, all day, He waits sublime,
Until the fulness of the time
  Decreed from his eternity.

REVE DU MIDI.

.

F. Juengling

REVE DU MIDI.

BY ROSE TERRY.

HEN o'er the mountain steeps,
 The hazy noontide creeps,
 And the shrill cricket sleeps
  Under the grass;
 When soft the shadows lie,
 And clouds sail o'er the sky,
 And the idle winds go by,
With the heavy scent of blossoms as they pass, —

 Then, when the silent stream
 Lapses as in a dream,
 And the water-lilies gleam
  Up to the sun;
 When the hot and burdened day
 Rests on its downward way;
 When the moth forgets to play,
And the plodding ant may dream her work is done, —

 Then, from the noise of war,
 And the din of earth afar,
 Like some forgotten star
  Dropt from the sky, —
 The sounds of love and fear,
 All voices sad and clear,
 Banished to silence drear, —
The willing thrall of trances sweet I lie.

REVE DU MIDI.

Some melancholy gale
Breathes its mysterious tale.
Till the rose's lips grow pale
With her sighs ;
And o'er my thoughts are cast
Tints of the vanished past,
Glories that faded fast,
Renewed to splendor in my dreaming eyes.

As poised on vibrant wings,
Where its sweet treasure swings,
The honey-lover clings
To the red flowers —
So, lost in vivid light,
So, rapt from day and night,
I linger in delight,
Enraptured o'er the vision-freighted hours.

HOW ONE MAN WAS SAVED.

How One Man Was Saved.

BY AMANDA M. DOUGLASS.

I.

But love is indestructible. — Southey.

E WALKED slowly along that dusty highway, Mark Bradley, revolving many thoughts in his busy brain. A summer afternoon melting gradually into evening, a sun sinking behind the hill-tops, burnishing the spires with moulten gold. In the still atmosphere those trees were outlined against the crimson dappled sky with wonderful distinctness. Not a leaf stirred. Down the sloping sides wide stubble-fields took on a new glory. Here acres of grass, early mown, nodding a serene satisfaction over the comforting idea of a second crop. Cornfields turned yellow, the browned and faded tassels hanging listlessly on ripening stalks. A sort of lazy, over-ripe August picture.

Had it been never so beautiful he would not have paused to study it. He had other matters on hand. What was the paltry landscape to him? He could not make money out of it, and that was his whole thought by day and night. How many times he had walked over this road, dreaming of what awaited him at the end, hurried on with a buoyant step and hopeful heart. Now he lagged unconsciously, and when he came in sight of the gray cottages down yonder among the trees, he almost paused.

"She must know sometime," he said, and this thought urged him on.

The road began to wind downward. It grew shadier, and fragrant with spice of fir and pine. Here and there some wild asters starred it, or a spray of golden-rod. Common things, all. Dusty and dull. They fretted him strangely. How many times he had found this road lovely to look upon — the end delightful. He seemed to have outgrown it all at a bound.

Before he reached the cottage there was a little flutter at the door. A white dress, and the flash of a scarlet ribbon at the throat. A gleam of soft brown hair, just as the last reflection of sunset through the trees took it, and played about like an aureole.

She came to meet him, this little Janet Raeburn. An hour ago her face was worn and gray; every limb tired and overstrained, working at her machine. She had sighed wearily over the last long seam, shut down the cover with an impatient snap, hurried around with the supper things, and found at last a few brief moments in which to wash her face, comb out her brown hair, and change her dress. It had transformed her, or else the hope that brightened her cheeks; for now, coming out to meet her lover, she looked really pretty.

He scanned her face earnestly. A broad, low forehead, small but irregular features, a mouth compressed by emotions or trials to a firmness and reticence rarely seen in two-and-twenty. He fancied, and perhaps rightly enough, that she was growing old and worn. He was in a mood to note these things, so she had put on her smiles and brightness in vain.

He took the little hands in his and kissed her. Then he held her quiet for a moment and sighed.

"What is it, Mark?"

She had a low, smooth, cool voice. One pleasant to hear in a sick-room, or at any time of great trial. As if one would like to hear her pronounce a benediction over this dying summer day.

"Let us walk out here. I am stifled all day with that hot, smothering air in the shop! It almost makes me hate to enter a house."

She was a trifle surprised at his vehement tone.

They took the edge of the soft, short grass, as it was too early yet for dew, down as far as the great sycamore tree, back again, and all in silence.

Janet studied his face furtively. It was gloomy and impenetrable. Of late he had been unlike himself. She tried to make him talk; but at first he responded only in monosyllables. And then she returned to the old query, —

"What is the matter, Mark?"

"Sit down here," and he paused at a great stone by the road-side, "for I have much to tell you, Janet."

She looked at him wonderingly.

"I am going away."

A woman would have skirmished about this fact, and broken it by degrees, to make the suffering less for the listener. He, being a man, went straight to the point at once.

She studied him with her brown eyes. There was something in the fearless scrutiny that made him wince.

"Why?" She could not trust herself to any longer sentence, for the blow seemed to have struck some vital part.

"I'll tell you why. I've been a fool for weeks and weeks. I've beat about the bush and staved off the truth, when I ought to have spoken. I am tired and sick of this dragging life. The same, month in and month out. If a man was a stick or stone he might be satisfied to go on the treadmill round. But I am not. Life isn't endurable on such terms!

His enunciation was rapid, his voice hoarse with dull passion.

"I thought you had a good situation, Mark?"

"Good enough, I suppose, as the matter goes; but I'm tired of drudgery. A man just keeps soul and body together. If one saves up a few dollars, the machinery's out of gear, and all hands off for a week or two. Or orders don't come in. Something continually to drain a man of his last cent. So there's nothing ahead, nothing between one and starvation, if an unlucky stroke should befall him. It frets me to death!"

"What can you do?"

"I'll show you what I can do, some day. I mean to be a rich man, Janet;" and he brought his clenched fist down on the rock with a force that numbed his fingers.

"O Mark," she said, with a little cry, "wealth doesn't always bring happiness."

"Don't take up that cant; I'm sick and tired of it. I'd risk wealth bringing me happiness. All I want in this world is money. With that will come everything else. And why have not I as good right to it as any other person? When I see these men riding around in their carriages, dressed in broadcloth and fine linen, giving sumptuous dinners, their houses perfect palaces of elegance, I *am* filled with envy. Why, their very servants have an easier life than mine!"

"I believe God gives us what is best." She spoke slowly, but in a steady tone.

"No, you *can't* think it, Janet. The clergymen preach about it on Sundays, and some weak, deluded people hug a sort of martyr belief to their hearts and glory in it. As if for every evil here, every misfortune, every loss, some great gain was to be met with in that other and fabulous country."

A bitter, bitter fear smote Janet Raeburn's heart. How many times she had trembled at the half-knowledge that this man affected to sneer at a Supreme Ruler.

"You can't think it," he went on with more vehemence. "Is it right that you, a weak and frail woman, should have the care of a bedridden mother and a feeble old father who is as much charge as a child? There is your brother and his wife taking their pick of everything, making money, scrimping and squeezing until the very stones cry out. See how they are prospered while you are working yourself to death! Is there any justice in that? Is God pleased to see you tried and worn, and worried, here in your youth, when everything should be bright and restful? No, I don't believe it. Here's the world and here's the struggle. Strong souls win, and I mean to dare it."

In the earlier days of their acquaintance she used to argue. More than once it seemed as if she had almost persuaded him. But he had always gone back to his old scepticism; so she had trusted to the future day of love. Would it ever come? For now she felt tired and faint-hearted. She, with her woman's eyes, saw how he could have lightened her burdens; but she would sooner die than thrust them upon him.

"So I am going away. I've had it planned for several weeks, and been putting off the announcement in a cowardly fashion. I knew how the separation would hurt you. If it could be, I'd take you with me. God knows I shall miss you sorely. But I'm bound to get above this stagnant level. I'll have enough to satisfy my wants without grovelling like a dog from Monday morn until Saturday night.

"What will you do?" How curiously calm her voice was.

"I've some brains and a tolerable education. There's a

friend of mine in New York who has made a good deal of money one way and another. He was in town a month ago, and wanted me to join him in some ventures. It's just the life I should like — hurry, excitement, something for your pains. I've saved up a little, and I mean to double it, quadruple it,— make a fortune, in short."

"And, then —?"

"I'll come back for you."

She stood up straight and firm before him. The twilight was falling now, and making purple shadows at the edges of the trees. Her white dress looked almost ghostly, but her eyes were unnaturally bright.

"No, Mark," she said, "you will not come back for me then. You think so now, — I'll do you that justice; but in the new life, when wealth and station and refinement are yours, I should be an unsightly blot, — mar the picture with my plainness, my worn face, my tired heart. You will need youth and grace and beauty."

"Do you doubt me, — my truth, my honor?"

He rose, too, then, and folded his arms across his broad chest. How proud she had been of him! How many times she had nestled to that bosom, been folded in those arms! Forgive her if she had longed for the time when it would be her home, her shelter. She felt so utterly lost and forlorn without him, and yet he seemed to be drifting rapidly away from her. She could make no answer.

"The old, stale romance," he said with a little sneer. "You don't give me much credit in fancying it."

"I shall not be fit for you then." Her voice was low and sad.

He walked up and down past her. He hated to have her doubt him, for he was so confident of his own strength.

"No," he went on, "I want you to believe, whatever comes,

that no woman can ever fill your place to me. I shall not be so weak after my struggle as to long for the youth and beauty that can be purchased with gold. And for your sake I want to be rich. To marry as men do, on precarious wages, and rear a family that may be doomed to beggary by another's whim, is what I could never do. And to go on waiting year after year in this fashion — "

Something roused her strangely. A fire flashed into the eyes and the pale cheeks.

"And I want *you* to believe," she said in a strong, clear tone, "that poverty has no terrors for me, — that work is no hardship : it was my birthright. I feel as if I should distrust any life that was easy and luxurious."

He laughed a trifle scornfully.

" Well," he said, "when I come back a rich man, reject me if you will, but now do not refuse me your love. Some of your true believers pretend to look upon woman's love as a sort of safeguard in an evil hour. So don't deprive me of this strength. "

His words cut deeply into her heart; but for all that, she came to him, leaned her throbbing head against his shoulder. He could not see the tears that overflowed her eyes.

They both paced the rapidly darkening path in silence. Once, as they neared the cottage, she said, —

" You will come in ? "

" Not to-night, Janet. I must go back immediately."

" When shall you leave ? "

" Next week. Monday is pay-night. It will be a relief not to drudge at the old toil any more."

" And what you mean to do, Mark, is perfectly honest and honorable ? "

He laughed scornfully.

" Janet," he said presently, " the world isn't as you think it.

These overstrained virtues do not pay in a great city, or anywhere, if a man means to get along. This high, theoretical
honesty sounds well enough in a book or a sermon, — people
are paid for writing and preaching it; but it never made the
listeners rich, that I heard. How much of it do your church
members carry into business? They're sharp enough, Heaven
knows!"

He had taunted her more than once, lately, in this manner.
She turned now.

"I do not know that the treachery of Judas was ever considered a better deed because he was one of the disciples," she
said in a strong, sad tone, almost coming to tears.

"We will not quarrel when there is a prospect of a long
separation before us. I shall be out on Sunday evening.
Good-night!" and he kissed her tenderly.

She stood in the dusk for many minutes after he had left
her, but not following out her first impulse — which was to
weep. For it seemed as if she must gird herself anew now.
Down the long future, somewhere, there would be plenty of
time for weeping.

II.

JANET RAEBURN entered the cottage at length.
Hastily lighting a candle, she ran up to her room
and pulled off the white dress she had put on with
so much pride an hour or two ago. Then she arranged her mother comfortably for the night, roused her
father from his nap on the rude settle, and sent him to bed as
if he had been a child. After being sure that everything
was safe, she retired once more to the room where she had

dreamed many a sweet young dream. Her life had always been hard, but being glorified these two years by Mark Bradley's love, had made it seem at times positively delightful. She had thought *if* Mark would marry her, and come there to live, share the profits of the farm with her brother John!— for it would easily afford them both employment. She had ventured to hint this to him.

"It wouldn't do, Janet," he said, "John would look upon me as an interloper. We don't like each other any too well now. He's your brother; but I must say he and his wife are close-fisted, grasping people, and he's bound to get all he can out of the farm. It would be more sensible for you to marry me and go away. The old folks are as much his parents as they are yours, and it is as much his place to do for them. I haven't much of a start, to be sure, but you are welcome to it. We would get along somehow."

Leave her parents to the care of Martha Raeburn, who regarded every moment wasted that was not devoted to money-getting! No, she could never do this. They were young and would wait.

And yet the waiting appeared to stretch itself out indefinitely.

When John Raeburn married, he had built a cottage quite at the upper end of the farm, being urged to the step by Martha, who had said, and wisely, they would be better friends apart. They worked the farm, and took the profits, supplying the old people so scantily that Janet, a handy little seamstress, bought a machine in order to render herself more independent of them. John was a loud and dogmatic talker, and whenever Janet tried to appeal to brotherly kindness, he invariably fell back upon the fact that he and Martha slaved from morning till night — and what did they have but a living? "I should be a good deal the gainer if I hired a farm for myself," he said; but, in her heart of hearts, Janet believed if he really thought so he would do it. Her very soul revolted at his meanness and selfishness.

It had come to be an accepted fact between the lovers that Janet's duty was here for the present. And since Mark Bradley had been smitten with this fever for wealth he had cared less for marriage. Poor Janet's heart died within her. Was the whole world going mad in a thirst for wealth?

Janet Raeburn prayed fervently that night. She had a sort of blind faith, if you will, that in the darkest hour God would not let his storms overwhelm her. Some way it would come out right in the end. But the waiting was so long, so hard! She had been trying to solve Mark's doubts, to lead him to the same belief that stayed her soul in hours of trial. But even here she had failed. And now he was going away!

There seemed to be a great deal of unfinished work in the world. Toil left off before fruition was reached, thwarted plans, people getting into wrong paths for want of some friendly hand to guide them aright. How perplexing it all was!

If she could have married Mark six months ago! John was counting on his father's death, impatient for a division of the property. She could see how this would simplify matters, and Mark would not object to having one invalid with them. There would be money enough to start him in some business, and then the restlessness, the sort of kicking against fate that embitters him so, would be over. Now and then this thought crept into her heart, but she strove to banish it. It tempted her cruelly this night. For, if Mark went away, who would guide him in a new home?

A weak man, you say! Well, the most of us are weak. Now and then a temptation touches us like a galvanic shock,

revealing the vulnerable spot. We thrust it out of sight, but
there in the darkness and loneliness it does not heal to sound,
solid flesh, although we tell ourselves it will. Blind always,
until we turn into the narrow path where God's light makes
it a new day.

In some intuitive way Janet understood this weakness of her
lover's. He was not a mean man — he would have cut off
his right hand sooner than stoop to the petty deeds whereby
John Raeburn managed to screw another dollar out of the
estate. He would not have defrauded his employer out of ten
minutes. Honesty in all little matters was ingrained in him.
But he had a restless, dissatisfied nature; he hated to be one
of the plodders; he smarted under the airs men with money
gave themselves, and wanted to be on the higher social plane
where he would not have them to endure.

Janet was helpless, and could only pray. Somehow, God
would not fail to bring it all out right. Though he had
listened for over eighteen hundred years, he was not weary.
And believing this, she fell asleep.

Friday, Saturday, and then Sunday. What long, long
days they were! Janet performed all her duties with a silent
air and grave face. Her poor old mother noticed this. But
not until Monday did Janet announce the separation that was
in store for her.

Mrs. Raeburn, too, had accepted the fact that Janet could
not marry. Perhaps the most bitter trial of all was the knowledge that no one considered it specially hard for her.

"He's a smart young fellow, Janet, and I think it's a sensible move. Now, while he has no incumbrance, he can live
cheaply and go anywhere he likes, and if he means to make
anything, it is best for him to attempt it while he's young and
strong. Two or three years won't seem much to you now."

That was her mother's comfort. Indeed, she wished *her*

husband had been more energetic and ambitious in his young days; but he had always taken life too easy.

John commended the plan also, and proposed he and Martha should come over to tea at Mark's last visit. And so when Mark found he had suited them all he began to take heart, though he had told himself before, that it was a mean shame to go off and leave Janet to struggle alone.

"I'm right glad," Martha said, walking home with her husband. "Janet will stay contented now. If she'd married, I don't know what we *should* have done, for I couldn't have taken care of your mother and father, and hiring a nurse is so expensive. It would have eaten up the whole estate."

Somehow John and Martha Raeburn seemed to have an impression that these old people, in living on, wronged them. Not that either would have put it in so many words, but Martha always said to her neighbors: "It's so hard to have the old folks sick and helpless," as if it increased her labors and cares.

Janet Raeburn took up her burden, making no moan. These evenings with Mark had been such an indescribable comfort to her — the only bright spots in her life. Heaven only knew how hard and weary it was for the girl. The whirr of the machine sounded pleasantly to her at last, because in its noise she could not think. So, between sewing, nursing and housework, her days went on slowly, and it was a pleasure to know they were past. Then, Mark's letters were a solace; though they were often brief.

He came to visit her the next summer. He had been successful beyond his anticipations. He had improved so much in his bearing and manner; for instead of the slow, thoughtful look, his eyes were bright and keen, his air brisk, his clothes jaunty and stylish, and the whole man seemed to have undergone some potent change.

He felt how hardly the twelve months had used Janet. He knew now that he could win fairer and fresher women, with hundreds where she would have but a penny. And in a discouraged mood, one day, she offered him his freedom.

I think it would have been a temptation to any man situated as he was, — as they both were. And I am glad I can tell you, in spite of the little struggle, his love for her had the true ring.

"Janet," his voice was husky with emotion, "never say such a thing to me again. Do you take me for a villain, child? To leave you in this loneliness, in this toilsome round, with no hope to count on, — no, I am not so bitterly cruel."

She came to his arms and wept some happy tears. Thank God that she had something to remember at a later day.

"If I could take you away from it all, and see you growing bright again."

"Not now," she said softly, willing to wait.

That winter her mother died, and her father was stricken with paralysis. John and Martha moaned over the hard fate, but offered little assistance. Old Mr. Raeburn was really less trouble than his wife, for he was neither querulous nor impatient, so Janet's burden did not seem any heavier. At last the end came, and it was summer again; but one of those seasons that fill men's hearts with dread, for a pestilence was stalking forth through the land.

In this quiet country place they scarcely dreaded the cholera. Even in the town, two miles beyond, there had been but few sporadic cases, not sufficient to drive the inhabitants wild with apprehension.

"Of course," Martha Raeburn said, walking home from the funeral, "the property'll have to be divided. You'll buy out Janet's part."

"The old house isn't worth anything," John mused. "I've

worked the ground up pretty well. The days and days I've spent over it! And now, I suppose, Janet will want the increased value. It's hard when a man's worked so! If it hadn't been for me, the farm would not be worth half what it is. Father always was a poor manager."

"Let's take Janet home with us. It's best to talk the matter over with her before that Bradley puts her up to anything. He's mighty fond of a good bargain."

"Yes," John said. So Janet, utterly worn out, was glad of the kindly invitation.

After she ate her supper she begged them to excuse her.

"Don't go to bed yet, Janet; I want to have a little talk. There are some things we may as well settle between ourselves."

"Not to-night, John," and her pale lips quivered.

"I am sure you can sit up in this easy-chair," interposed Martha. "I often drop down into it, and it rests me as much as going to bed."

"You are very kind, but I can't talk to-night; I'm so tired. To-morrow must do."

Martha ungraciously attended her to the spare room, to take off the best pillows and remove the counterpane. "I've such lots of work to do that I have to be careful," she said, in a complaining tone; and as she went downstairs she grumbled to John, "If Mark had been here, she could have walked up and down the road half the night with him."

"I'll take her first thing in the morning. I want the business settled before Bradley can come on."

Janet cried herself to sleep in five minutes. But it hardly seemed as many more before some one burst into the room with a shriek.

"Janet, for Heaven's sake, come down. I believe John's been taken with the cholera."

Janet Raeburn groped her way along the stairs as if she were half blind. The old clock in the sitting-room struck three. The candle was flaring on the table, and in the chamber beyond, John, the strong man, was groaning in mortal agony. Janet did all she could in a wild, dazed way, and then went for the doctor. What if it was night? — she was not afraid.

At noon the next day John Raeburn died. Martha was in a panic of the wildest terror. She blamed Janet; she declared if old Mr. Raeburn had not died just as he did all would have gone well with John. It was his grief and his overwork. And now she was to be left destitute and alone; for she knew she could only hold a paltry third of what was coming to her husband. But she need not have worried. Two days from the burial of John Raeburn, they "carried her out also."

For many weeks after that Janet lay as if in a dream. Not conscious of pain or anxiety, too weak even to have a wish, and with not mind enough to express it even if she had. A peaceful rest for both body and soul was that low fever. But she came out of it at length, and began to think about herself and one other. Good Dr. Miles had taken her home in the beginning of her illness, and his wife cared for her in a manner quite new to the forlorn girl. Yet she wondered why they watched her so, and why they gave each other such sorrowful looks. Surely she was getting well. If Mark would only write. It was three months since she had heard from him. She had written him the second letter in answer to his, detailing her father's death and that of John. That was nearly two months ago. And so she told Dr. Miles every day to look for a letter, but he always came back empty-handed. What did it mean?

"I know Mark too well to think he would be false to me," she said, proudly, one day.

The doctor winced.

"What is it?" she began. "You know something. He is not dead? I couldn't bear that, after all the rest."

"Better a hundred times if he was, God knows!" Dr. Miles said hoarsely.

"What *can* be worse?" She came and looked into his face with curious calmness.

"There *are* worse things, child, and he's done one of 'em. He's a villain, and it's good you found it out so soon."

Janet could think of but one thing. "I want you to know," she said, proudly, "that more than a year ago I offered him back his freedom. He was so bright and handsome, and life looked so fair before him, while I was always in a black shadow. He wouldn't take it, but I've hardly considered it an engagement since."

"I'm glad you're a little weaned off. For, Janet, child, he's a felon in state prison.

The soft eyes dilated with incredulous horror, at first. The lip quivered, the very limbs shook, as she moaned,—

"Oh, no, no, you are mistaken!"

He took a paper out of his desk, and showed her the paragraph. Five years in state prison! The room whirled round, and it seemed as if she were dying. Then she roused herself, and asked what he did.

"Embezzled funds — no, that wasn't it, either. He took some money that didn't belong to him, to speculate with, and the thing went to smash. His partner ran away, but then he pleaded guilty, so the matter was clear enough. You're young, Janet, and you're coming into a good property; so forget the scamp."

She went out of the room without another word. Dr. Miles did not like the stony calm into which she settled, but he never had the heart to discuss the matter again.

The Raeburn farm was sold in two parcels. Little did John or Martha imagine the end, while they were toiling so relentlessly. And Janet Raeburn found herself mistress of seven thousand dollars. The interest would support her in the simple fashion in which she chose to live.

She went on with Dr. Miles for a year, but all the while she was slowly working out a plan that haunted her, day and night. And then she left them for some cousins, who lived in the State of Delaware, and who urged her to make them a visit. She had another motive in view. She went to New York, and sought out the man Mark Bradley had defrauded. And after hearing all the particulars, she offered him her fortune, and promised to assume the remainder, three thousand dollars, if he would interest himself in procuring a pardon for Mark.

"I declare, I never was so touched in my life," Mr. Cummings said to his lawyer. "I don't know but she might have convinced me that he was a positive hero, if she had tried. And, Thorpe, she absolutely means to marry him. She is sure she can save him. I don't know but we were pretty hard on him. I meant it to teach others a lesson as well. There's too much of this speculating, and making haste to be rich. If you can do anything for him —"

"Do you mean to take the money?" the lawyer asked, with a curious expression.

"Do you think me a Jew usurer, Thorpe? The money? Why, I'd as soon take a pound of her flesh! No, if she can make a good man of him, she'll be a missionary, the like of which you won't see more than once in your lifetime. She's nearer an angel than many of them will be in heaven."

One day Mark Bradley cast off his prison clothes, and walked tremblingly through the long corridor to the reception-room. Why Mr. Cummings should interest himself in his behalf was a great mystery. He was to meet him now, and his lip twitched nervously, his face flushed with shame, that he *could* have wronged so noble a man.

The figure that turned upon him was not Mr. Cummings's. With the first glance he staggered back to the door-post, his whole frame weak at the very sight. She came nearer — Janet Raeburn.

"Don't," he exclaimed, brokenly; "go away, Janet. The one thing I prayed most fervently for was that you should forget me."

"Mark," she answered, "in your prosperity you didn't desert me."

LADY WENTWORTH.

LADY WENTWORTH.

BY NORA PERRY.

HE shall marry me yet!" he smiling said —
Smiling, and under his breath — but red
As flame his dark cheek glowed, and bale-fire burned
In his passionate eyes, as he swiftly turned

Out of the sunshine into the shade —
Out of the sunshine she had made
But a moment before — this girl with a face
Whose very frown had a winsome grace,

They used to swear, in that old, old time,
When her beauty was in its wonderful prime,
When her laughing eyes of golden brown
Were the toast and rage of Portsmouth town,

Of Hampshire's Portsmouth, there by the sea,
Where the Wentworths ruled and held in fee
Half the country-side of rock and shore,
For a hundred and fifty years or more.

"She shall marry me yet!" 'Twas the Wentworth blood
That rose up then in that turbulent flood —
The Wentworth purpose that under his breath
Would hold to its passionate will till death.

"She shall marry me yet!" And down he strode
Across the pathway, across the road,
With a firm quick step and a firm quick heart,
To work his will and to play his part.

And a difficult part it was to play,
For the Wentworth blood ran either way —
His mother's blood that held him tied
By kinsman bonds on either side.

LADY WENTWORTH.

But as mother's blood leaves stronger trace
Than father's blood in a turbulent race,
It may have been that his wilful way
Had the stronger current to move and sway.

At all events, as the months wore on
And no tidings came from her cousin John
To the beautiful toast of Portsmouth town,
The Wentworth temper rose up to drown

The passionate Wentworth love in her breast,
And the Wentworth pride helped on the rest:
And six months after her laughing scorn
Of her dark-eyed suitor, suing forlorn,

She stood by his side one autumn day
A beautiful bride: he had won his way;
But the gossips said that a bride never wore
In Portsmouth town such a look before.

Seven years after, John Wentworth came
Back to his home with a foreign fame:
Back he came to rule and to reign,
As the Wentworths had ruled and ruled again,

From father to son, in Hampshire State.
Seven years after — why he tarried so late —
So late and so long in a foreign land,
Was a riddle not easy to understand.

Yet late as he came, a welcome burned
In a hundred hearth-fires. Wherever he turned
A hand stretched out and a smile awaited
This kinsman of theirs so long belated.

But amid this lavish neighborly cheer
He missed a face he had once held dear.
" My Cousin Frances : where doth she hide?"
He questioned at last. " She watches beside

A sick man's bed — a good nurse, I should say,
To keep the blue-devil baliffs away."
That night John Wentworth knocked at the door
Of his cousin's house. A foot on the floor,

LADY WENTWORTH.

A whisper of silk, and there she stood.
In that moment John Wentworth's cousinly mood
Melted away like frost at the fire.
He thought he had killed the old desire;

He thought that love and hate both lay
Slain by the past at that long late day;
He thought — but what matters it now
The thought that *had* been, when on cheek and brow

Flames the signal-torch from his wakened heart?
What matters it now the cousinly part
He had fancied was his, when on his pulses beat,
With that swift, wild throb, as their glances meet?

But he curbed the Wentworth temper awhile,
As he bent in greeting, and hoped, with a smile,
That he found her well. Hearing the state
Of her good man's health, he could not wait

His cousinly sympathy to convey.
A tedious illness he had heard them say:
But the town was eloquent of her care,
Which had certainly left her no less fair

Than he remembered her seven years since —
He turned a moment as he saw her wince —
Turned, and with a purpose fell,
In a sneering, passionate tone, " Ah, well,

Women, we know, have a potent charm
To ward themselves from trouble and harm — "
She caught the sneer, and stayed him there,
With a passionate cry: how did he dare,

Who had played so falsely these seven long years,
To fling at *her* feet his idle sneers?
" *I* false!" He laughed. " Madam, where went
Those fine love letters I foolishly sent

Across the seas in those old, old days?
I waited long — 'tis a pretty amaze
You feign, my cousin — I waited long
For a word or a sign, for my faith was strong

227

In that old, sweet time ; but the months went by,
And never a line came back, and I
Still clung to my faith, till a morning in May
There came to me news of a wedding day

Here in Portsmouth town, and the bride
Was the girl who had stood at my side
And sworn to be mine, six months before —
You shiver, my cousin : the wind from the shore

Blows harshly to-night." A gesture here
Checked his bitter reproach, his menacing sneer,
And a hoarse voice cried, "John Wentworth, wait
Ere you dower me with the dower of hate.

No letter of yours from over the sea
In that old, old time came ever to me :
Day after day the months went by —
Day after day, and what was I

But a maiden scorned? Day after day
The months went by; when I heard them say
That John Wentworth staid
To woo and to win an English maid.

My spirit rose like our swift shore tide —
' Twas the Wentworth temper, the Wentworth pride —
And — your cousin and mine had wooed me long :
His love was sure, and my hate was strong —

Quick, passionate hate for the suitor fine,
The false, false gallant who over his wine
Could pledge new loves while the old love waited,
Faithful and fond, this lover belated."

" Sweetheart!" Back she started in swift affright
At this fond, bold cry, and the red turned white
In her oval cheek. A moment more,
And swiftly striding across the floor,

This lover belated, who missed his bride
Seven years ago, is at her side ;
And the fond, bold voice on her listening ear,
On her listening heart, over every fear,

LADY WENTWORTH.

Like a rising river, gains and gains,
While unreckoned, unheeded, the swift night wanes,
Till the clock strikes twelve on the landing stair;
Then John Wentworth turns with a gallant air,

And embraces his cousin as a kinsman may,
Though all the gossips be looking that way.
Yet his parting words, whispered low in her ear,
Were never meant for a gossip to hear.

But long before the spring had come
To Portsmouth shores, in many a home
The gossips' tongues were making bold
With the Wentworth name; and the story told,

Which ran through the town like a breath of flame,
Was this — that John Wentworth never came
To his cousin's house but by signal or sign,
A silken scarf or a kerchief fine

Flung out of the casement, or at night
In the western window a candle's light.
And the gossips, observant, would smile, and say,
" So! the sick man sleeps at this hour of the day ! "

Or at evening, when the candle flares
In the western window, " Dame Frances' cares
Are over early, it seems, to-night."
If Dame Frances caught this bale and blight

Of the gossips' tongues, little she recked :
No Wentworth yet was ever checked
By a gossip's tongue, however bold.
But there comes a day when the kerchief's fold

Is missed at the casement, and that night
No candle flares its signal-light.
When another morning dawns again
The tolling Portsmouth bells explain

The missing candle, the kerchief fine.
Dame Frances now of signal or sign
Has little need; in the chamber there,
Where a sick man yesterday claimed her care,

229

LADY WENTWORTH.

A dead man lies in solemn state;
And peering at the linen and plate
Downstairs, the neighbors, under their breath,
Talk of the sick man, and his death;

Of the widow's prospects; and one more bold
Hints that ere the year's grown old
The Wentworth mansion across the way
Will have a mistress fine and gay.

But ere a month had passed of the year,
All the seamstresses far and near,
In and out of Portsmouth town,
Were sewing fast at a wedding-gown

Of brocaded satin, foreign and rare,
For Dame Frances Atkinson to wear.
"Shame!" cried the gossips, far and wide,
And "Shame!" cried the Wentworths in their pride —

All the Wentworth kin in Hampshire State.
This haste was unseemly; she'd only to wait
In her widow's weeds a year and a day,
And not a gossip could say her nay.

Then up she spoke, this wilful dame —
Scornfully spoke, with a tongue of flame:
"Seven years I have served the Wentworth pride;
Seven years with a Wentworth courage lied

To the world with my smiling face,
To find at the end — no sovereign grace
To save my soul, but a curse alone,
The curse of a lie that shamed my own!

Cheated and tricked seven weary years,
Won by a lie — no lying tears
Have I to waste, no time to wait
On the man who dies seven years too late!"

Scared and shocked, the Wentworths stared
At this reckless dame, whose passion dared
To cast at the dead man, scarcely cold
In his fresh-turned grave, these accusals bold.

LADY WENTWORTH.

Sacred and shocked, but never a word
Of ban or blame was ever heard
From their lips again, and come the day
When my lady Wentworth, fine and gay,

Reigned in the Wentworth mansion there,
Not a gossip in Portsmouth but spoke her fair.
But under their breaths, when twilight fell,
Under their breaths, they would sometimes tell

The old, old story of signal and sign,
The candle flame, and the kerchief fine;
And under their breaths would croak a fear
That my lady had lent but too willing an ear

To the evil whispered against the dead,
The doubtful tale so suddenly sped
From mouth to mouth, while for yea or nay,
Helpless and dumb the dead man lay.

But never upon my lady's face,
Never a doubt showed sign or trace,
As she looked the curious gossips down
In the little world of Portsmouth town —

Never a doubt from year to year,
Never a doubt, and never a fear;
For whatever the truth of the troubled past,
My lady had come to her own at last!

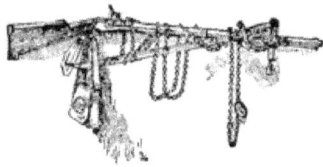

THE IRON BLACKSMITH.

.

THE IRON BLACKSMITH.

FROM "ALL THE YEAR ROUND."

OLD England she has great warriors,
    Great princes and poets great;
But the blacksmith is not to be quite forgot
    In the hist'ry of the State.
He is rich in the best of all metals,
    Yet silver he lacks and gold;
And he payeth his due, and his heart is true,
    Though he bloweth both hot and cold.
Then hurrah for the iron blacksmith!
    And hurrah for his iron crew!
And whenever we go where his forges glow,
    We'll sing what a man can do.

The boldest is he of incendiaries
    That ever the wide world saw,
And a forger as rank as e'er robb'd the bank,
    Though he never doth break the law.
He hath shoes that are worn by strangers,
    Yet he laugheth and maketh more;
And a share conceal'd in the poor man's field,
    Yet it adds to the poor man's store.
Then hurrah for the iron blacksmith!
    And hurrah for his iron crew!
And whenever we go where his forges glow,
    We'll sing what a man can do.

235

AN HOUR
AT CHRIST'S HOSPITAL.

An Hour at Christ's Hospital.

BY WM. MATHEWS.

Author of " Getting on in the World."

MONG the strange and unique sights which attract the eye of the stranger in London, one of the oddest is the apparition, in the neighborhood of Newgate street, of a boy dressed in a monastic garb of the sixteenth century. It is raining, yet he is bareheaded, and he wears a long, flowing, dark-blue coat, like a monk's tunic, confined at the waist by a leather belt, which, with yellow breeches, shoes, and yellow stockings, complete his quaint costume. Who is he? Is he the ghost of some boy of the sixteenth century, or is he a living, flesh-and-blood urchin of the nineteenth, arrayed in the garb of a bygone time? We need not be ashamed to confess our inability to solve this problem, for it is one which puzzled even so acute and ingenious a thinker as Sydney Smith. The witty canon of St. Paul's brooded long over the origin of the Blue-Coat boy,—for it is by this name he is yclept, — and finally hazarded the theory that he was a Quaker in the chrysalis state.

"Look at the circumstances," he urged in a discussion with the Countess of Morley; "at a very early age, young Quakers disappear, — at a very early age the Coat-Boys are seen; at the age of seventeen or eighteen young Quakers are again seen, — at the same age the Coat-Boys disappear. Who has ever heard of a Coat-Man? The thing is utterly unknown in natural history. That such a fact should have escaped our naturalists is truly astonishing. . . . Dissection would throw great light on the question; and, if our friend ———— would receive two boys into his house about the time of their changing their coats, great service would be rendered to the cause. I have ascertained that the Blue-Coat infants are fed with Drab-Colored pap, which looks very suspicious." To these daring speculations Lady Morley replied with reasonings equally shrewd and hard to answer. The possible correctness of Sydney's theory she admitted; but there was a grave difficulty: "The Blue-Coat is an indigenous animal, — not so the Quaker. . . . I have seen and talked much with Sir R. Ker Porter on this interesting subject. He has travelled over the whole habitable globe, and has penetrated with a scientific and scrutinizing eye into regions unexplored by civilized man, and yet *he* has never seen a Quaker baby! He has lived for years in Philadelphia (the national nest of Quakers); he has roamed up and down, broadways and lengthways, in every nook and corner of Pennsylvania, and yet he never saw a Quaker baby; and what is new and most striking, — never did he see a Quaker lady in a situation which gave hope that a Quaker baby might be seen hereafter. This is a stunning fact, and involves the question in such impenetrable mystery as will, I fear, defy even your sagacity, acuteness, and industry to elucidate."

How the question was settled — whether Sydney continued to maintain that there never was such a thing as a Quaker baby, that "they are always born broad-brimmed and in full quake" — we know not; and therefore, in lieu of other authority, we will accept Traditional History of the Blue-Coats. According to this, Christ's Hospital, or the Blue-Coat School, was founded in 1553 by Edward VI., just before

his death. "I do know," said the dying king, then but sixteen years old, "that there be those who love to learn, even
as I their King, and yet who cannot, for they be poor. Therefore will I do that this day which shall keep my memory
green." The buildings were provided on the site of the monastery of the Gray-Friars, of which a few arches, a part of a
cloister, are all that remains ; and the queer costume of the
boys, which they intensely dislike, was adopted at the time.
The flat caps supplied to them are so small that the boys
rarely wear them, and go bareheaded. In 1672, Charles II.
founded the Mathematical School for forty boys, called
"King's Boys," to which twelve more have been added, and
they are distinguished by a badge on the shoulder. The
school now has an income of £40,000 a year, and it feeds,
clothes and educates twelve hundred children, of whom five
hundred, including the younger children and girls, are kept
in a branch school at Hertford for the sake of pure air. Four
boys annually are sent from it to the Universities. On New
Year's Day the "King's Boys" are presented at Court; on
Easter-Monday all the boys walk in procession to the Royal
Exchange ; on Easter-Tuesday they visit the Lord Mayor ;
and on St. Matthew's Day they deliver orations in their hall
before the Mayor, Corporation and Governors. Like many
other noble charities in England, this has been wrested from
its original purpose, and many pupils gain admission upon
other pleas than poverty.

It was through the kindness of Messrs. Trübuer & Co., the
celebrated publishers and booksellers, whose shop on Ludgate
Hill, London, is within a stone's throw of Christ's Hospital,
that we found an "Open Sesame" to the famous school. While
indulging our bibliomaniac propensities there one day, we
were so lucky as to be introduced to Dr. Brette, Professor of
Modern Languages in the school, who kindly invited us to

visit it the next day.   Christ's Hospital!   Where is the
scholar or literary man whose pulse does not quicken at the
mention of these words?   What a crowd of pleasant memories they conjure up!   Who that has skimmed but the surface
of modern English literature, has not read Charles Lamb's
charming "Recollections" of that shool?   Christ's Hospital!
where not only the loving *Carlagnulus*, as he was afterwards
called, but Coleridge, "the inspired charity-boy," and Cam-
den, and Leigh Hunt, and scores of other worthies, were in-
ducted into the mysteries of the three R's, "Reading, 'Riting,
and 'Rithmetic," — how did our heart leap up at the prospect
of seeing the very benches which they hacked, the very spots
where they quailed under the eagle glance and thunder tones
of Boyer!

Accepting Dr. B.'s invitation, we next day proceeded to
Newgate street, and passing the gloomy prison, turned into a
cross street, where, about noon, we entered the boy-King's
school.   Entering a corridor, we notice on the wall numerous
tablets, placed there in honor of the graduates of the school
who have become its benefactors.   Not a few of England's
"solid men" of business, who were educated here, have left
handsome legacies to the institution.   The buildings consist
of several large structures of brick, fronting paved courts,
which serve as playgrounds for the boys in sunny weather,
while the corridors shield them from the rain in wet weather.
Following the lead of Dr. Brette, we visit a school-room,
where the hard seats and benches, with deep gashes testifying
to the excellence of English cutlery, remind us of the pine
planks upon which we tried our Rogers in the old red school-
house of our boyhood.   Was there ever a schoolboy who
did not make his mark with his jack-knife, whatever his
failures in recitation?

The eulogists of "modern improvements" will find but little

to admire in these venerable piles, except the swimming-room — the water of which is tempered at pleasure — the admirable bathing-rooms, of which the boys are required to make use at prescribed times — and the clean and airy hospital, where boys who are unwell, or have met with an injury in their sports, are cared for by skilful surgeons and tender nurses. Visiting these apartments, we next glance at the dormitories, with their multitude of iron bedsteads, and the monitor's room in the corner; and then return to the playground, whose memory is busy calling up the history of the Blue-Coats whose names have been blazoned high on the scroll of fame. Can it be, we musingly ask ourselves, that the spider-legged, spectral-looking " Elia " once trod these courts, and trembled in yon room under the master's frown? Did Horne Tooke here begin the " *Diversions* of Purley," and Wesley shout in his boyish games as he never did afterwards in the Methodist class-room? Did the thoughtful Addison and the careless, impulsive Dicky Steele here kick the football, and little Barrow begin the pugilistic feats which he afterwards repeated with such effect in his struggle with an Algerine corsair? Was it here that the youthful Blackstone tested in boyish games the strength of the British Constitution, and was it from this school that Mitchell, the translator of Aristophanes, was translated to Cambridge? All these names are on the muster-rolls of the Blue-Coat School, and many others hardly less brilliant.

We think of these, and of the Bedlam cells to which naughty boys in Elia's time were consigned: little fellows of seven years shut up all night in these dungeons, where they could just lie at length upon straw and a blanket; with only a peep of light by day, let in from a prison-orifice at the top; and permitted to come forth only twice a week, and then to be flogged by the beadle. We think of the fierce master, Boyer, and his two wigs, — the one serene, smiling, fresh-powdered, and betokening a mild day; the other, an old, discolored, unkempt, angry caxon, denoting frequent and bloody execution. We see him shaking his knotty fist at a poor trembling child, and crying, "*Sirrah, do you presume to set your wits at me?*" —then flinging back into his lair, and after a few moments bounding forth again, and singling out a lad with the exclamation, "Od's my life, sirrah, I have a great mind to whip you;" which imperfect sense he speedily "pieces out," as if it has been some Devil's Litany, with the expletory yell, "and *I* WILL, *too*." We see the "gentle Elia" in another room, where the thunders rolled innocuous, listening to the *Ululantes*, and catching glimpses of Tartarus; we hear Coleridge, hardly yet in his teens, unfolding the mysteries of Plotinus, or reciting Homer or Pindar in his Greek, to the wonderment of the visitors. We think, too, of Coleridge's pious ejaculation when told that his old master was on his death-bed, "Poor J. B.! may all his faults be forgotten, and may he be wafted to bliss by little cherub boys all head and wings, with no *bottoms* to reproach his sublunary infirmities!" We think of the poor scholar who conveyed to his room his fragments of coarse meat, which he was supposed to sell to beggars, for which he was excommunicated by the other boys as a *gag-eater*, until the kind steward found that he carried home the scraps, which he denied himself, to his starving parents. We think of the silver medal which the noble lad received for this from the governor of the school; and then, perhaps, our thoughts revert to another boy, the petty Nero, afterwards seen a culprit in the hulks, who actually branded a boy who had offended him, with a red-hot iron, and who nearly starved forty younger lads, by exacting from them, daily, one-half of their bread to pamper a young ass which he had contrived to smuggle in and keep upon the leads of the *ward*, as the dormitories were called, till the foolish beast, waxing fat, and kicking in the fulness of bread, betrayed him by braying. All these and many other recollections, comic or touching, are related by Lamb and Coleridge in their own inimitable style, but hardly seemed to us, when we were 4000 miles away, as they do now, realities.

It was here, too, that the following ludicrous scene occurred, narrated by some graduate, to omit which, in an account of this famous school, would be like blotting Moses' experience from the Vicar of Wakefield : —

Among the scholars when Lamb and Coleridge attended was a poor clergyman's son by the name of Simon Jennings. On account of his dismal and gloomy nature, his playmates had nicknamed him "Pontius Pilate." One morning he went up to the master, Dr. Boyer, and said, in his usual whimpering manner, " Please, Dr. Boyer, the boys all call me Pontius Pilate." If there was one thing which old Boyer hated more than a false quantity in Greek and Latin, it was the practice of nicknaming. Rushing down among the scholars from his pedestal of state, with cane in hand, he cried in his usual voice of thunder, " Listen, boys ! the next time I hear any of you say ' Pontius Pilate ' I'll cane you as long as this cane will last. You are to say ' Simon Jennings,' not ' Pontius Pilate.' Remember that, if you value your hides." Having said this, Jupiter Tonans remounted Olympus, the clouds still hanging on his brow. Next day, when the same class were reciting the catechism, a boy of remarkably dull and literal turn of mind had to repeat the creed. He had got as far as "suffered under," and was about popping out the next word, when Boyer's prohibition unluckily flashed upon his obtuse mind. After a moment's hesitation he blurted out, "Suffered under Simon Jennings, was cruci"—The rest of the word was never uttered; for Boyer had already sprung like a tiger upon him, and the cane was descending upon his unfortunate shoulders like a Norwegian hail-storm or an Alpine avalanche. When the irate Doctor had discharged his cane-storm upon him, he cried, "What do you mean, you booby, by such blasphemy?" "I only did as you told me," replied the simple-minded Christ-Churchian. "Did as I told you," roared old Boyer, now wound up to something above the boiling point. "What do you mean?" As he said this, he again instinctively grasped his cane more furiously. "Yes, Doctor; you said we were always to call 'Pontius Pilate' 'Simon Jennings.' Didn't he, Sam?" appealed the unfortunate culprit to Coleridge, who was next to him. Sam said nought; but old Boyer, who saw what a dunce he had to deal with, cried, "Boy, you are a fool. Where are your brains?" Poor Dr. Boyer for a second time was floored, for the scholar said, with an earnestness which proved its truth, but to the intense horror of the learned potentate, "In my stomach, sir." The Doctor always respected that boy's stupidity ever after, as though half afraid that a stray blow might be unpleasant.

But whoop! Our musings are interrupted by shouts, and away bounds a football, followed by an avalanche of boys, screaming, pushing, kicking, jostling, and tumbling headlong, very much like boys in America; and showing by their earnestness, impetuosity, and energy, that they belong to the nineteenth century and not to the sixteenth. But what a plague their long coats are, and how strange that the governors do not see the grotesqueness and inconvenience of these old monkish costumes! To play their games the boys tuck up their coat tails; and so, we suppose, will have to do for years to come, till John Bull can see that modern garments may be substituted without impairing the stability of the British Constitution.

But, hark! a burst of martial music is heard; the boys have dropped the footballs, and, under the directions of a drill-master, are marshalled in platoons, each displaying its number on a flag. After a series of evolutions, they march, seven hundred strong, with a boy-band of thirty performers at their head, up the grand staircase to the Gothic Hall, to dinner.

This magnificent hall, which was completed in 1829, is one hundred and eighty-seven feet long, is lighted by large stained-glass windows, has an organ-gallery at one end, and the walls are hung with portraits of the founder and benefactors of the institution. We take seats on a platform on the west side of the hall; a bell is touched, and a boy at the organ plays an anthem, while seven hundred children's voices mingle in the chant of thanksgiving. Another bell, and down sit the boys, off come the covers, and Blue-Coats wait on Blue-Coats, until all have quieted their barking stomachs with a plentiful supply of meat, potatoes and bread, and, above all, beer. In Elia's day, the provision made for the "inner man," or rather "inner boy," was very step-motherly. The dinner, on several days, consisted only of milk "por-ritch," blue and tasteless, with rice milk and pease-soup that was decidedly coarse and choking. The attenuated small-beer was poured from leathern jacks, and tasted of the vessel it had been kept in.

After their plain repast, the boys, themselves, clear the tables; and after a few minutes' chat with them, we leave the hall, with many thanks to Dr. Brette for his courtesies, and a feeling that henceforth the writings of *Carlagnulus* and the "Highgate Sage" will have for us an added charm, — if it is possible for us to hang with profounder interest over their bewitching pages. Meanwhile, if any of our readers care to see the famous old school as it has been for three centuries, they must cross the ocean soon, for these venerable piles are speedily to be swept away, to make room for the ruthless locomotives of the Mid-London Railway.

THE ELM AND THE VINE.

The Elm and the Vine.

FROM THE SPANISH OF JOSE ROSAS, OF MEXICO.

BY WILLIAM C. BRYANT.

PHOLD my feeble branches
  With thy strong arms, I pray:"
Thus to the Elm, her neighbor —
  The Vine — was heard to say;
" Else, lying low and helpless,
  A weary lot is mine;
Crawled o'er by every reptile,
  And browsed by hungry kine."
The Elm was moved to pity;
  Then spoke the generous tree:
" My hapless friend, come hither,
  And find support in me."
The kindly Elm, receiving
  The graceful Vine's embrace,
Became, with that adornment,
  The garden's pride and grace;
Became the chosen covert
  In which the wild birds sing;
Became the love of shepherds,
  And glory of the Spring.

Oh, beautiful example
  For youthful minds to heed!
The good we do to others
  Shall never miss its meed;
The love of those whose sorrows
  We lighten shall be ours,
And o'er the path we walk in
  That love shall scatter flowers.

THE SCENE-PAINTER'S WIFE.

THE SCENE-PAINTER'S WIFE.

BY M. E. BRADDON,

Author of "Lady Audley's Secret," etc.

OU wouldn't think it, to look at her now, sir," said the old clown, as he shook the ashes out of his blackened clay, " but madam was once as handsome a woman as you'd see for many a long day. It was an accident that spoilt her beauty."

The speaker was attached to a little equestrian company with which I had fallen in during a summer day's pedestrianism in Warwickshire. The troupe had halted at a roadside inn, where I was dawdling over my simple mid-day meal, and by the time I had smoked my cigar in his companionship, the clown and I were upon a footing of perfect friendliness.

I had been not a little struck by the woman of whom he spoke. She was tall and slim, and had something of a foreign look, as I had thought. Her face was chiefly remarkable for the painful impression which it gave to a stranger. It was the face of a woman who had undergone some great terror. The sickly pallor of the skin was made conspicuous by the hectic brightness of the large black eyes, and on one cheek there was a scar — the mark of some deadly hurt inflicted long ago.

My new friend and I had strolled a little way from the inn, where the rest of the company were still occupied with their frugal dinner. A stretch of sunny common lay before us, and seemed to invite a ramble. The clown filled his pipe, and walked on meditatively. I took out another cigar.

"Was it a fall from horseback that gave her that scar?" I asked.

"A fall from horseback! Madame Delavanti! No, sir, that seam on her cheek was made by the claws of a tiger. It's rather a curious sort of story, and I don't mind telling it, if you'd like to hear it; but for the Lord's sake don't let her know I've been talking of her, if you should happen to scrape acquaintance with her when you go back to the inn."

"Has she such a dislike to being talked about?"

"I rather think she has. You see she's not quite right in the upper story, poor soul; but she rides beautifully, and doesn't know what fear means. You'd scarcely believe how handsome she looks at night when she's dressed for the ring. Her face lights up almost as well as it used to do ten years ago, before she had the accident. Ah, she was handsome in those days, and used to be run after by all the gentlemen like mad! But she never was a bad lot, never — wild and self-willed, but never a wicked woman, as I'll stake my life. I've been her friend through thick and thin, when she needed a friend, and I've understood her better than others.

She was only twelve years old when first she came to us with her father, a noted lion-tamer. He was a man that drank hard now and then, and was very severe with her at such times; but she always had a brave spirit, and I never knew her to quail before him or before the beasts. She used to take her share in all the old man's performances, and when he died, and the lions were sold off, our proprietor kept a tiger for her to perform with. He was the cleverest of all the animals, but a queer temper, and it needed a spirit like Caroline Delavanti's to face him. She rode in the circus as well as performing with the tiger, and she was altogether the most valuable member of the company, and was very well paid for her work. She was eighteen when her father died, and within a year of his death she married Joseph Waylie, our scene-painter.

I was rather surprised at this marriage, for I fancied Caroline might have done better. Joe was thirty-five if he was a day — a pale, sandy-haired fellow, not much to look at, and by no means a genius. But he was awfully fond of Caroline. He had followed her about like a dog ever since she came among us, and I thought she married him more out of pity than love. I told her so one day; but she only laughed, and said: —

"He's too good for me, Mr. Waters, and that's the truth. I don't deserve to be loved as he loves me."

The newly-married couple did indeed seem to be very happy together. It was a treat to see Joe stand at the wing and watch his wife through her performances, ready to put a shawl over her pretty white shoulders when she had done, or to throw himself between her and the tiger in case of mischief. She treated him in a pretty, patronizing sort of way, as if he had been ever so much younger than her instead of twelve years her senior. She used to stand on tiptoe and kiss him before all the company sometimes at rehearsal, much to his delight. He worked like a slave in the hope of improving his position as he improved in his art, and he thought nothing too good for his beautiful young wife. They had very comfortable lodgings about half a mile from the manufacturing town where we were stationed for the winter months, and lived as well as simple folks need live.

Our manager was proprietor of a second theatre, at a seaport town fifty miles away from the place where we were stationed; and when pantomime time was coming on, poor Joseph Waylie was ordered off to paint the scenery for this other theatre, much to his grief, as his work was likely to keep him a month or six weeks away from his wife. It was their first parting, and

257

the husband felt it deeply. He left Caroline to the care of an old woman, who took the money, and who professed a very warm attachment for Mrs. Waylie, or Madame Delavanti, as she was called in the bills.

Joseph had not been gone much more than a week when I began to take notice of a young officer who was in front every evening, and who watched Caroline's performance with evident admiration. I saw him one night in very close conversation with Mrs. Muggleton, the money-taker, and was not over-pleased to hear Madame Delavanti's name mentioned in the course of their conversation. On the next night I found him loitering about at the stage-door. He was a very handsome man, and I could not avoid taking notice of him. On inquiry I found that his name was Jocelyn, and that he was a captain in the regiment then stationed in the town. He was the only son of a wealthy manufacturer, I was told, and had plenty of money to throw about.

I had finished my performance earlier than usual one night soon after this, and was waiting for a friend at the stage-door, when Captain Jocelyn came up the dark by-street, smoking his cigar, and evidently waiting for some one. I fell back into the shadow of the door, and waited, feeling pretty sure that he was on the watch for Caroline. I was right. She came out presently and joined him, putting her hand under his arm, as if it were quite a usual thing for him to be her escort. I followed them at a little distance as they walked off, and waited till I saw Joe's wife safe within her own door. The captain detained her on the doorstep talking for a few minutes, and would fain have kept her there longer, but she dismissed him with that pretty, imperious way she had with all of us at times.

Now, as a very old friend of Caroline's, I wasn't going to stand this sort of thing; so I taxed her with it plainly next day, and told her no good could come of any acquaintance between her and Captain Jocelyn.

"And no harm need come of it either, you silly old fellow," she said. "I've been used to that sort of attention all my life. There's nothing but the most innocent flirtation between us."

"What would Joe think of such an innocent flirtation, Caroline?" I asked.

"Joe must learn to put up with such things," she answered, "as long as I do my duty to him. I can't live without excitement, and admiration, and that sort of thing. Joe ought to know that as well as I do."

"I should have thought the tiger and the horses would have given you enough excitement, Caroline," I said, "without running into worse dangers than the risk of your life."

"But they don't give me half enough excitement," she answered; and then she took out a little watch in a jewelled case, and looked at it, and then at me, in a half-boastful, half-anxious way.

"Why, what a pretty watch, Carry!" said I. "Is that a present from Joe?"

"As if you didn't know better than that!" she said. "Country scene-painters can't afford to buy diamond watches for their wives, Mr. Waters."

I tried to lecture her, but she laughed off my reproaches; and I saw her that night with a bracelet on her arm, which I knew must be another gift from the captain. He was in a stage-box, and threw her a bouquet of choice flowers after her scene with the tiger. It was the prettiest sight in the world to see her pick up the flowers and offer them to the grim-looking animal to smell, and then snatch them away with a laugh, and retire, courtesying to the audience, and glancing coquettishly towards the box where her admirer sat applauding her.

Three weeks went by like this, the captain in front every

night. I kept a close watch upon the pair, for I thought that, however she might carry on her flirtation, Joe's wife was true at heart, and would not do him any deliberate wrong. She was very young and very wilful, but I fancied my influence would go a long way with her in any desperate emergency. So I kept an eye upon her and her admirer, and there was rarely a night that I did not see the captain's back turned upon the door of Mrs. Waylie's lodgings before I went home to my own supper.

Joe was not expected home for another week, and the regiment was to leave the town in a couple of days. Caroline told me this one morning with evident pleasure, and I was overjoyed to find she did not really care for Captain Jocelyn.

"Not a bit, you silly old man," she said; "I like his admiration, and I like his presents, but I know there's no one in the world worth Joe. I'm very glad the regiment will be gone when Joe comes back. I shall have had my bit of fun, you know, and I shall tell Joe all about it; and as Captain Jocelyn will have gone to the other end of the world, he can't object to the presents — tributes offered to my genius, as the captain says in his notes."

I felt by no means sure that Joseph Waylie would consent to his wife's retaining these tributes, and I told her as much.

"Oh, nonsense," she said; "I can do what I like with Joe. He'll be quite satisfied when he sees Captain Jocelyn's respectful letters. I couldn't part with my darling little watch for the world."

When I went to the theatre next night, I found the captain standing talking to Caroline just inside the stage-door. He seemed very earnest, and was begging her to do something which she said was impossible. It was his last night in the town, you see, and I have very little doubt that he was asking her to run away with him — for I believe the man was over head and ears in love with her — and that she was putting him off in her laughing, coquettish way.

"I won't take your answer now," he said very seriously. "I shall wait for you at the door to-night. You can't mean to break my heart, Caroline; the answer must be yes."

She broke away from him hurriedly. "Hark," she said, "there's the overture; and in half an hour I must be upon the stage."

I passed the captain in the dark passage, and a few paces farther on passed some one else whose face I could not see, but whose short, hurried breathing sounded like that of a person who had been running. We brushed against one another as we passed, but the man took no notice of me.

Half an hour afterwards I was lounging in a corner of the ring while Caroline went through her performances with the tiger. Captain Jocelyn was in his usual place, with a bouquet in his hand. It was New-Year's night, and the house was very full. I had been looking all round for some time, when I was startled by the sight of a face in the pit. It was Joseph Way-lie's face, ashy pale and fixed as death — a face that meant mischief.

"He has heard something against his wife," I thought. "I'll run round to him directly I can get out of the ring, and make matters square. Some confounded scandal-monger has got hold of him, and has been poisoning his mind about Caroline and the captain." I knew there had been a good deal of talk in the theatre about the two — talk which I had done my best to put down.

Captain Jocelyn threw his bouquet, which was received with a coquettish smile, and a bright upward glance that seemed to express profound delight. I knew that this was mere stage-play; but how must it have looked to the jealous man, glaring with fixed eyes from his place at the back of the pit! I turned to

look at him as the curtain fell upon the stage, but he was gone.
He was going round to speak to his wife, no doubt. I left the
ring immediately, and went to prepare her for the interview,
and, if needful, to stand between her and her husband's anger.

I found her at the wing, trifling with her bouquet in an absent
way.

"Have you seen Joe?" I asked.

"No," she answered. "He hasn't come back, has he? I
didn't expect him for a week."

"I know, my dear; but he was in front just now, looking as
pale as a ghost. I'm afraid some one has been talking to him
about you."

She looked rather frightened when I said this.

"They can't say any harm of me, if they speak the truth,"
she said. "I wonder Joe didn't come straight to me, though,
instead of going to the front of the house."

We were both wanted in the ring. I helped Caroline through
her equestrian performance, and saw that she was a little nervous and anxious about Joe's return. She did not favor the
captain with many more smiles that evening, and she told me
to be ready for her at the stage-door ten minutes before the
performance was over.

"I want to give Captain Jocelyn the slip," she said; "but I
dare say Joe will come to me before I'm ready."

Joe did not appear, however, and she went home with me. I
met the captain on my way back, and he asked me if I had been
seeing Mrs. Waylie home. I told him yes, and that her husband had come home. Joe had not arrived at the lodgings,
however, when Caroline went in, and I returned to the theatre
to look for him. The stage-door was shut when I went back;
so I supposed that Joe had gone home by another way, or was
out drinking. I went to bed that night very uneasy in my mind
about Caroline and her husband.

There was an early rehearsal of a new interlude next morning, and Caroline came into the theatre five minutes after I got there. She looked pale and ill. Her husband had not been home.

"I think it must have been a mistake of yours about Joe," she said to me. "I don't think it could have been him you saw in the pit last night."

"I saw him as surely as I see you at this moment, my dear," I answered. "There's no possibility of a mistake. Joe came back last night, and Joe was in the pit while you were on with the tiger."

This time she looked really frightened. She put her hand to her heart suddenly, and began to tremble.

"Why didn't he come home to me?" she cried, "and where did he hide himself last night?"

"I'm afraid he must have gone out upon the drink, my dear"

"Joe never drinks," she answered.

While she stood looking at me with that pale, scared face, one of our young men came running towards us.

"You're wanted, Waters," he said shortly.

"Where?"

"Upstairs in the painting-room."

"Joe's room?" cried Caroline. "Then he has come back. I'll go with you."

She was following me as I crossed the stage, but the young man tried to stop her.

"You'd better not come just yet, Mrs. Waylie," he said in a hurried way, that was strange to him. "It's only Waters that's wanted, on a matter of business." And then, as Caroline followed close upon us, he took hold of my arm and whispered, "Don't let her come."

I tried to keep her back, but it was no use.

"I know it's my husband who wants you," she said. "They've

been making mischief about me. You shan't keep me away from him."

We were on the narrow stairs leading to the painting-room by this time. I couldn't keep Caroline off. She pushed past both of us, and ran into the room before we could stop her.

"Serve her right," muttered my companion. "It's all her doing."

I heard her scream as I came to the door. There was a little crowd in the painting-room round a quiet figure lying on a bench, and there was a ghastly pool of blood upon the floor. Joseph Waylie had cut his throat.

"He must have done it last night," said the manager. "There's a letter for his wife on the table yonder. Is that you, Mrs. Waylie? A bad business, isn't it? Poor Joseph!"

Caroline knelt down by the side of the bench, and stopped there on her knees, as still as death, till the room was clear of all but me.

"They think I deserve this, Waters," she said, lifting her white face from the dead man's shoulder, where she had hidden it; "but I meant no harm. Give me the letter."

"You'd better wait a bit, my dear," I said.

"No, no; give it to me at once, please."

I gave her the letter. It was very short. The scene-painter had come back to the theatre in time to hear some portion of that interview between Captain Jocelyn and his wife. He evidently had believed her much more guilty than she was.

"I think you must know how I loved you, Caroline," he wrote; "I can't face life with the knowledge that you've been false to me."

Of course there was an inquest. We worked it so that the jury gave a verdict of temporary insanity, and poor Joe was buried decently in the cemetery outside the town. Caroline sold the watch and the bracelet that Captain Jocelyn had given her, in order to pay for her husband's funeral. She was very quiet, and went on with the performances as usual a week after Joe's death, but I could see a great change in her. The rest of the company were very hard upon her, as I thought, blaming her for her husband's death, and she was under a cloud, as it were; but she looked as handsome as ever, and went through all her performances in her old, daring way. I'm sure, though, that she grieved sincerely for Joe's death, and that she had never meant to do him wrong.

We travelled all through the next summer, and late in November went back to Homersleigh. Caroline had seemed happier while we were away, I thought, and when we were going back, she confessed as much to me.

"I've got a kind of dread of seeing that place again," she said; "I'm always dreaming of the painting-room as it looked that January morning with the cold light streaming in upon that dreadful figure on the bench. The room's scarcely been out of my dreams one night since I've been away from Homersleigh; and now I dread going back as if — as if *he* was shut up there."

The room was not a particularly convenient one, and had been used for lumber after Joe's death. The man who came after him didn't care to paint there by himself all day long. On the first morning of our return, Caroline went up and looked in at the dusty heap of disused stage furniture and broken properties. I met her coming away from the room.

"O Mr. Waters," she said to me with real feeling, "if he had only waited to hear me speak for myself! They all think I deserved what happened, and perhaps I did, as far as it was a punishment for my frivolity; but Joe didn't deserve such a fate. I know it was their malicious talk that did the mischief."

I fancied after this that her looks changed for the worse, and that she had a kind of nervous way in going through her equestrian performances, as if there was a fever upon her. I couldn't judge so well how she went through the tiger act, as I was never on the stage with her, but the brute seemed as submissive as ever. On the last day of the year she asked our manager to let her off for the next night. "It's the anniversary of my husband's death," she said.

"I didn't know you were so precious fond of him," he answered, with a sneer. "No, Mrs. Waylie, we can't afford to dispense with your services to-morrow night. The tiger act is one of our strong features with the gallery, and I expect a full house for New Year's night."

She begged him very hard to let her off, but it was no use. There was no rehearsal on New Year's morning, and she went to the little cemetery where Joe was buried, a three miles' walk, in the cold and rain. In the evening, when she came to the wing her eyes were brighter than usual, and she shivered a good deal more than I liked to see.

"I think I must have caught cold in the cemetery to-day," she said to me when I noticed this. "I wish I could have kept this night sacred — this one night — to my husband's memory. He has been in my mind so much to-day."

She went on, and I stood at the wing watching her. The audience applauded vociferously, but she did not make her accustomed courtesy; and she went about her work in a listless way that was very different from her usual spirited manner. The animal seemed to know this, and when she had got about half-way through her tricks with him, he began to respond to her word of command in a sulky, unwilling manner, that I didn't like. This made her angry, and she used her light whip more freely than usual.

One of the tiger's concluding tricks was a leap through a garland of flowers which Caroline held for him. She was kneeling in the centre of the stage with this garland in her hands, ready for the animal's spring, when her eyes wandered to

the front of the house, and she rose suddenly with a shrill scream,
and her arms outstretched wildly. Whether the sulky brute
thought that she was going to strike him or not, I don't know;
but he sprang savagely at her as she rose, and in the next moment she was lying on the ground helpless, and the audience
screaming with terror. I rushed upon the stage, with half-a-
dozen others, and we had the brute muzzled and roped in a few
breathless moments, but not before he had torn Caroline's cheek
and shoulder with his claws. She was insensible when we carried her off the stage, and she was confined to her bed three
months after the accident with brain-fever. When she came
among us again, she had lost every vestige of color, and her
face had that set look which you must have observed just now.

"The fright of her encounter with the tiger gave her that
look," I said. "I don't much wonder at it."

"Not a bit of it," answered the clown. "That's the curious
part of the story. She didn't think anything of her skirmish
with the tiger, though it quite spoilt her beauty. What frightened her was the sight of her husband sitting in the pit, as he
had sat there a year before, on the night of his death. Of
course you'll say it was a delusion, and so say I. But she declares she saw him sitting amongst the crowd — amongst them,
and yet not one of them, somehow, with a sort of ghastly light
upon his face that marked him out from the rest. It was the
sight of him that made her drop her garland and give that
scream and rush that frightened the tiger. You see she had
been brooding upon his death for a long time, and no doubt she
conjured up his image out of her own brain, as it were. She's
never been quite the same since that fever; but she has plenty
of pluck, and there's scarcely anything she can't do now with
Baber, the tiger, and I think she is fonder of him than of any
human creature, in spite of the scar on her cheek."

MY COUSIN EMILY.

My Cousin Emily.

BY J. F. WALLER,

Author of " Mogdalena, The Spanish Duel."

I.

IN the greenwood tangles
 Of a lordly park,
Where bright flowers, like spangles,
 Deck the verdure dark ;
Where, from out the branches,
Many a sweet bird launches,
Blithest music, filling
All the air with trilling —
 Finch and thrush and lark —

II.

There's a beech-walk shady,
 Gravelled trim and neat,
Where a little lady
 Trips with tiny feet,
Onward still advancing,
Like a fairy dancing,
And her blue eyes beaming
With a childlike gleaming
 Marvellously sweet.

III.

Ivy-leaves entwining
 Auburn hair enfold —
Just like emeralds shining
 In a shrine of gold.
And her loose robe flowing
As she sways in going,
Like the waves of ocean,
With the merry motion,
 To and fro 'tis rolled.

IV.

On she trips, as lightly
  As the gleesome kid;
And her eyes shine brightly
  From each long-fringed lid,
As she stops a minute,
Listening to the linnet,
Or to watch the shining
Of the lizard, twining
  In the grass half-hid.

V.

Till at length she reaches
  Where the greenwood maze
Breaks from out the beeches
  To the morning rays;
And the autumn lustre
Plays upon a cluster
Of bright leaves and flowers,
Falling down in showers
  From an antique vase.

VI.

There, amid the splendor
  Of rich flowers and rare,
Stands that maiden tender —
  Herself a flower most fair.
O'er the vase she's stooping,
With her large eyes drooping,
Till her cheek reposes
'Mid the flushing roses
  Gathering round her there.

VII.

But, 'mid all this blooming —
  Rose and eglantine,
And the rich perfuming
  Of sweet Jessamine —
'Mid bells of purple fuchsias —
'Mid honeysuckle luscious —
One flower still is wanting,
Greatest of Nature's granting:
  No *passion-flower* is seen.

MY COUSIN EMILY.

VIII.

Ah! that little maiden
  Still is fancy-free,
With no love yet laden —
  Light and bright is she.
Lips that ne'er knew sobbing,
Heart ne'er wildly throbbing,
Eyes ne'er swol'n with weeping,
Sleepless vigils keeping —
  My cousin Emily.

IX.

Yet, sure as morning brightens
  Into noonday hour,
And sure as May-bloom whitens,
  And fruit succeeds the flow'r,
So sure will Love yet find thee —
So sure his fetters bind thee.
Ah! may'st thou then step lightly,
And look as fair and brightly
  As now in yonder bower!

STARLIGHT.

STARLIGHT.

BY CELIA THAXTER.

THE chill, sad evening wind of winter blows
    Across the headland, bleak and bare and high,
Rustling the thin, dry grass that sparsely grows,
    And shivering whispers like a human sigh.

The sky is thick with stars that sparkle keen.
    And great Capella in the clear northeast
Rolls slowly up the cloudless heaven serene,
    And the stern uproar of the sea has ceased.

A fleeting moment, and the earth seems dead —
    So still, so sad, so lonely, and so cold!
Snow-dust beneath me, and above my head
    Star-dust in blackness, like thick-sprinkled gold.

The stars of fire, the tiny stars of ice,
    The awful whirling worlds in space that wheel.
The dainty crystal's delicate device —
    One hand has fashioned both — and I, who kneel

Here on this winter night. 'twixt stars and snow,
    As transient as a snowflake and as weak,
Yearning like all my fellow-men to know
    His hidden purpose that no voice may speak, —

In silent awe I watch his worlds : I see
    Mighty Capella's signal, and I know
The steady beam of light that reaches me
    Left the great orb full seventy years ago.

A human lifetime ! Reason strives in vain
    To grasp at time and space, and evermore
Thought. weary grown and baffled. must again
    Retrace its slow steps to the humble door

STARLIGHT.

Of wistful patience, there to watch and wait
  Devoutly, till at last Death's certain hand,
Imperious, opens wide the mystic gate
  Between us and the future He has planned.

Yea, Death alone.   But shall Death conquer all?
  Love fights and pleads in anguish of despair.
Sooner shall great Capella wavering fall,
  Than any voice respond to his wild prayer.

And yet, what fire divine makes hope to glow
  Through the pale ashes of our earthly fate?
Immortal hope, above all joy, below
  All depths of pain wherein we strive and wait!

Dull is our sense! hearing we do not hear,
  And seeing, see not; yet we vaguely feel
Somewhere is comfort in the darkness drear,
  And, hushing doubts and fears, we learn to kneel.

Starlight and silence!   Dumb are sky and sea,
  Silent as death the awful spaces lie;
Speechless the bitter wind blows over me,
  Sad as the breathing of a human sigh.

SIGHTS AND HUMORS.

SIGHTS AND HUMORS OF THE WALLED CITY AND ENNISKILLEN.

BY JAMES M. BAILEY,

(The Danbury News Man.)

I.

LONDONDERRY — AN IRISH POLICEMAN.

FROM Port Rush I went to Enniskillen, by way of Londonderry. I stopped at Londonderry two or three hours, to see the old city wall. If I am not disastrously mistaken, Londonderry is the only city in the United Kingdom boasting a complete wall about it. It is something to see a walled city. Aside from the wall, I do not know as there is anything of particular interest in Londonderry. It is a port for several American steamers, and is surrounded by bold scenery. It rained all the while I was there, which gave me an opportunity of seeing more of the people than I could have done on a pleasant day.

I will tell you how I saw the wall. I left the station and passed into a street of warehouses and dingy stores, with here and there an eating saloon. I stopped at a tobacco store for some cigars, and asked the proprietor for the address of the wall. He told me to keep on until I reached a broad, open thoroughfare. I would find the wall there. I kept on. When I got on the broad, open thoroughfare I saw opposite the blank side of a wall of masonry. Two arches pierced it, showing through each a vista of street. I knew that wasn't the wall, because it disappeared at each end in among buildings, and buildings towered above it on the other side. So I asked a policeman who stood under one of the arches to show me the wall, and he said that was the wall. And then the following conversation occurred between us : —

" Is there any way of getting up on it? " I asked.

" Yes. Are you a stranger? "

" I am. Is anybody allowed up on the wall? "

" You are not Irish, are you? "

" No," said I.

" English? "

" No. How do you get up on the wall? "

" Do you come from America? "

" Yes. How do you get up on the wall? "

" There is a stairway beyond. What part of America do you come from? "

" The Rocky Mountains. Is anybody allowed to go on the wall? "

· " Of course. How long have you been over? "

" Seven years. And now will you permit me to ask you a question? " I inquired, in some desperation.

" Of course."

" Thank you. Good day."

" Goo — good day," he stammered, in some surprise.

And thus we parted. Will we ever meet again? How solemn the thought.

I mounted a stairway which I found in a narrow street running from the arch and emptying into a public house, and was on the wall.

I do not know the exact date of the building of this work, but it had attained a fair age in 1688, when the famous siege occurred. It was built by the city of London, at an expense of

£11,000. The wall is of varying width, and consists of two exteriors of stone filled in with earth and cobbles. In some places two or three teams could drive abreast on it. However, they don't. But it is used as a promenade for the citizens. On the outer side is a battlemented guard of stone for the protection of troops operating on the wall. Houses and streets are built up against it, and the former so hide it that it is impossible to see any considerable portion of it, even when on it, at one glance.

There are guard-houses and bastions still remaining on it (the latter planted with flowers), which were once occupied by desperate and starving men, sacrificing for a principle, suffering for their religion.

What dreadfully bitter animosities are those which one Christian will entertain for another. What an awful thing it is to be a politician for Christ, rather than a lover of Him.

It is well known, perhaps, to my readers that the north of Ireland was the scene, some two hundred years ago, of great contention between the Catholics and Protestants. It was about this time that the Duke of York, who was James II., abdicated his throne, owing to the threatening aspect of his people, in favor of his daughter Mary, the wife of William, Prince of Orange, who was of the same nationality as the Eleventh Corps in the Army of the Potomac. In 1688, William and Mary landed in England, and were proclaimed King and Queen. Catholic Ireland favored James, and united with France to either restore him to the English throne, or to wrest Ireland from England and annex it to France. That little affair made the Battle of Boyne, the struggle at Enniskillen, and the heroic defence of Londonderry. The city was built and walled for the protection of the Protestants in the neighborhood. To give a history of Derry would require more time and patience than I can afford to devote to it. To simply give its events in chronological order would fill this entire volume.

At the close of 1688, the Protestant residents in the north of Ireland, favoring William and Mary, of course, became alarmed at the attitude of their Catholic neighbors, who were laying in pikes and cutlasses, or, to use a figure of speech, were rolling up their sleeves. They who were not already in the protection of the walls of Londonderry hastened there, and in 1689, in April, began the seige of the city by the combined Irish and French troops. It lasted 105 days, and so severe was it upon the city that nine thousand of its people perished from starvation, while scarcely a hundred were killed by the enemy's guns. An equal number of the foe perished from disease, and the effective firing of the men of Derry. It was finally broken by the arrival of provisions and troop-ships sent by the government. A clergyman named Walker made himself conspicuous in this defence, for bravery, eloquence and common sense.

Macaulay says: " Five generations have since passed away, and still the wall of Londonderry is to the Protestants of Ulster what the trophy of Marathon was to the Athenians. A lofty pillar, rising from a bastion which bore for many weeks the heaviest fire of the enemy, is seen far up and down the Foyle. On the summit is the statue of Walker, such as when, in the last and most terrible emergency, his eloquence raised the fainting courage of his brethren. In one hand he grasps a Bible. The other, pointing down the river, seems to direct the eyes of his famished audience to the English topmasts in the distant bay. Such a monument was well deserved ; yet it was scarcely needed ; for in truth the whole city is to this day a monument of the great deliverance. The wall is carefully preserved ; nor would any plea of health or convenience be held by the inhabitants sufficient to justify the demolition of that sacred enclosure which, in the evil time, gave shelter to their race and their religion."

Londonderry is near the head of a magnificent arm of the sea,

called Lough Foyle. Why the Scotch and Irish do not say
" Lake " rather than " Loch " and " Lough," is one of the mysteries that no man seems able to find out. Its houses rise, one
above the other to the summit, which is crowned by the cathe-
dral. A splendid Protestant college and model school adorns
Londonderry. It is called the Magee College, in honor of the
endower, Mrs. Magee, of Dublin.

II.

ENNISKILLEN — HOW THE IRISH PLAY BILLIARDS.

ATE in the afternoon I took the train for Enniskillen.
However much may be said in praise of the green
fields, beautiful lakes, and magnificent mountain
scenery of Ireland, precious little can be written in
compliment of the railway management. I remember waiting
once two whole hours to give a team time to return several
miles after an inspector whom the driver had neglected to bring
with him. One hundred people lost that two hours to accom-
modate one man too careless to attend to his own business.
When the inspector had arrived, and was seeing to some parcels,
I managed to stumble on a box and fall against him with sufficient force to knock him over a trunk. Several bystanders
remarked upon the singularity of the accident. It *was* singular.

The trains run in five hours about as far as corresponding
English trains do in three hours.

The ride to Enniskillen, sixty miles, was devoid of interest.
I reached Enniskillen shortly after dark, and took the 'bus to
the hotel. It was not an imposing building. An Irish writer
says the hotels of his country have improved seriously in the
past ten years. Before that time, he goes on to remark, there
were not two good hotels in the whole country. And so they

have improved in the last decade? I hope I feel sufficiently grateful for not having had to submit to the hospitality of an Irish hostelry previous to that time.

The Enniskillen hotel sat a good table, that is, the food was cooked well, as the extent of the table depends almost entirely on the taste and pocket of the guest. Its hallway was a narrow passage with a small opening in the right wall for a bar and office, a door opposite leading into a cramped and not particularly neat kitchen, *through which the billiard room was approached*, a stairway beyond the kitchen door, and a little smoking-room at the end of the passage. The bedrooms were in good condition and clean.

After supper I went into the billiard room. The evening was wet and chilly, and a fire was smouldering in the kitchen fireplace, before which sat two old women smoking pipes. Opposite the door I entered was a narrow, buttoned door which opened into the billiard room. This saloon was about fifteen by twenty feet, with a rather agitated floor, a low ceiling frescoed under the immediate auspices of a swarm of flies, and bare and dingy walls.

The billiard table was manned by two strapping young fellows, and the stable-boy was marking for them. He had just the position to please a boy — plenty to see and little to do.

The Irish play billiards with a vim that would be useful at a ruction. They are an impetuous people at any time, and do not seem to possess the faculty of restraint on needful occasion. These two fellows, and fine looking fellows they were, smashed the balls about with a velocity that was astonishing, and then swore every three minutes at their luck. I watched them for an hour, but seeing no abatement to their speed, I returned to the smoking room.

Enniskillen is on Lough Erne, the Killarney of Northern Ireland. The lake is about twenty miles in length and of varying width. At the widest part it is, I should judge, full six miles. It has a steamer, but it was not running when I was there, owing to a lack of patronage, although I offered to take passage if the owner would fire up. Half-way down the lake is a fine hotel, but its shutters were up, owing to a lack of patronage. I don't know when Lough Erne will pay in a commercial view, but it must first become popular before tourists will visit it. My little experience has taught me that people do not come to Europe to see the novel and beautiful, but the fashionable.

Thousands go to Killarney who never hear of Lough Erne, and yet, while Killarney is majestic, this is most beautiful.

Picture to yourself a lake of its size with three hundred and sixty-five islands dotting its surface, and nearly every one of them covered with foliage to the water's edge. Its shores are not high and rugged, and it lacks towering mountains to give it majesty, but it winds and twists about with romantic irregularity, and again widens out into a broad expanse as smooth as a mirror, while the distant isle appears like a castellated city of the olden time.

It is only by a row-boat that the trip is now made, and I took it in company with a gentleman from Pennsylvania, who was visiting Enniskillen at the time.

The propeller of the boat was a short and square-built man with a stout, peculiar white face, which denoted the presence of the strength of his people — consumption. No people live outdoors so much as the Irish, and no people suffer so much from this dreadful disease. And yet fresh air is its enemy. I doubted as I looked at him, that he would pull us through, but the doubt gave way to wonder before the trip was over. We pulled around the village — Enniskillen is on an island — and then through a tongue of water to the open lake. As we came out we passed, on the point of land to our right, a modern mansion with fine grounds, and, on that to the left, the broken walls of a

287

castle. It is called Portova Castle, from the fact that it stands at the point where those taking dead friends to Devenish island embarked in boats — Portova signifying " port of tears." We passed close to the castle, but there was no particular interest about it. Nothing but the four walls with massive turrets at at each angle now remain. Of all the gay and scheming, and good and bad, and hopeful and despairing, who have occupied it, none can boast as much balance as the old building, which could see nothing and hears nothing, can show.

III.

SPECULATIONS ON RUINS — A PAIR OF PENNSYLVANIA BOOTS.

WHEN you have got to this stage in your journey through Europe, you will have come to look upon ruins with about the same intensity of interest that you would contemplate pine-trees after a month's sojourn in Maine.

But it interesting to speculate on the origin of ruins. What puzzled me, when I heard of ruins afar off, was to understand how they became so — in what year, and what day, at what hour of the day, did they throw off the respectable yoke of usefulness, and sink into architectural loaferism? For two hundred years this castle has been a loafer — a corner-loafer at that. And why? Well, in the first place, it was built when protection against foes was as essential as protection against weather. It was not ornamented, it had no bay-windows, it was French-roofless. When civilzation so far advanced that every man was made safe in his possessions, and law usurped violence, the occupation of the building, its specialty, was done away with. It became a loafer, In some instances, as in that of Warwick Castle particularly, they were modernized and improved upon and are to-day in business and doing well. But in most cases they were deserted for more comfortable dwellings, and being too strongly built to be taken apart with economy, their walls were left. As for the wood-work, it was wrenched out for fuel; and as for the window-glass, where one could boast such a luxury, it was undoubtedly stoned out by the neighboring boys on Saturday afternoons. As to why the wood-work was not carefully removed and used in parts of the new structure, I would mention that it was mostly of oak, and most respectfully refer you for full information to some carpenter who has taken down an old oaken building, and undertaken to re-use the material. Anybody who has attempted to drive a cast-iron nail into a venerable oak board will be pleased to give you any information you may desire — if he is alive.

Sometimes the occupants were forced to skedaddle from the country, leaving the house tenantless, and the carpets of the victor not fitting the rooms of the deserted place, his wife would not consent to moving in; so the place was left to the tender mercies of poor and predatory neighbors.

It is easy enough to account for things when you sit right down and give your whole attention to them as I do.

As we moved up the lake, it grew wider, and in a few minutes we got breeze enough to warrant the boatman putting up the sail.

It was a nice breeze, and under its impulse we glided comfortably along. I took charge of the helm, and the Pennsylvanian wrapt himself up in his own reflections, which is a habit with Pennsylvanians, he told me.

Our main objective point was Devenish island, à place of ruins. Just before we reached it the boatman pointed to a clump of rushes growing up through the water near Devenish, and said that it was an island, although now submerged, and that once on a time a friar, being sore pressed by a horseman, jumped from Devenish to it, and saved himself.

This statement aroused the Pennsylvanian at once. He stood up in the boat and looked at the two points.

"Why," said he, "that is a distance of nearly one hundred feet; and do you mean to say, my man, that anybody ever jumped that?"

"Yes, sir," said the boatman, quietly.

"Did — did it strain him?" asked my companion, anxiously.

"I don't know, sir," answered the man; "but he did it, sir, an' I've offen heard it told."

"Well, I don't believe any man could jump that distance," stoutly asserted my friend — "unless," he shortly added, as a new light seemed to strike him, "unless he — he spit on his hands."

We ran the boat upon the beach, and landed. Devenish is an island of some twenty-five acres. It has not a tree or bush upon it, but it is covered with rank grass, a fact that is beautified by distance, two hours after a rain.

Devenish is the most important bit of land, viewed in connection with ruins, to be found in Ireland.

Its ruins consist of remains of a monastery, said to have been founded by St. Molaisse, *thirteen hundred years* ago; a round tower; a Great Church; a priory, and remains of earthen forts.

The item which made the greatest impression upon the Pennsylvanian was the height and liquidity of the grass. He had on a pair of Philadelphia fine boots, and by the time he reached the top of the ridge, every pore of those boots was drawing water; and, despite my expostulations, he swore he would return to the boat, and return he did. He said that he didn't care to die in a strange land, of inflammatory rheumatism.

But I pressed on, although I could feel the water souse in my boots at every step.

Of the ruins, I came first upon a church-tower, with its sustaining arch. This is the church. I picked my way over the fallen stones to beneath the arch, and found in one wing of it a stairway of stone, but was unable to ascend. A portion of a wall was standing, but there was nothing more left of the church. St. Molaisse's house is even less satisfactory to the tourist. But a small fragment of one of its walls remains. Not long ago it was in a complete state, and was then a low, stone-roofed, oblong building, with a door at one end. Having been built thirteen hundred years ago, it hardly seems possible that it could have been in good condition within the present century; but a glance at this fragment of wall, enormous in thickness, weakens skepticism. Some one must have demolished it, but who he could have been no one knows. He is safe, so far as I am concerned. A man who can tear down a building like that was will never be hunted by any of our family.

Near by his house, in a mound of earth, is the broken stone coffin of St. Molaisse, but of S. M. himself there is not a pinch. He is as if he never was. The lid to his coffin now forms a monument to some individual who is trying to snatch a few winks of sleep beneath his stolen property. He lies in the graveyard of the church, for the burial-place is still here, and is still in use. These British people can make a graveyard go further than we can. Cemeteries four and five hundred years old are common enough here. But in America, as soon as a graveyard gets a little old, we dig it up, and put down a new street in its place. Ten years after, some one comes along and wants his wife's uncle who had been laid there. No one knows what has become of the old gentleman, but every one tries to pacify the grief-stricken nephew. But he won't be consoled.

He dances around, and demands his uncle, and finally drags the town into a lawsuit.

The British are more reverential than we, and reap the benefit thereof.

The place is still used as a burial-ground, — this wild, lonesome spot, which nobody can reach without a boat, which has no fence about it to keep the cattle who pasture here from trampling over and befouling the graves. Saints and monks and holy men of all degrees have slept here, and as we are all our life trying to get into good company, it is but natural that the weakness should follow us to the grave.

As you can imagine, many of these graves are but simple clumps of earth, with no form to designate their nature. They are thick together, and I dare say they are frequently in layers, one above the other, and most of them are marked by a simple rough stone from the fields, without any mark upon them.

The round tower interested me more than any other object on the island. Round towers are peculiar to Ireland alone. I don't know how many there are of them here, but they are common. They are the best preserved of any stone-work left by the ancients. The gate posts in Ulster are sort of copies of the round towers. A round tower is from sixty to a hundred feet high, with a sharp conical roof, also of stone. You take a post and point one end of it, and you have the exact pattern of a round tower. It is built of dressed stone, laid so neatly together as to be symmetrical, and need no mortar. This one has an ornamented cornice around its eaves. But few do. It has a small opening for a door some eight or nine feet from the ground, and several openings above, which were probably used for windows. This tower, from the ground to the roof, is sixty-seven feet high, and the roof is sixteen feet in height. There were probably six floors to this tower, but how each was reached I am not able to explain, as the internal diameter of the tower is

only eight feet at the base, and but six and a half at the cornice.
Its base has a circumference of forty-nine feet, and its top forty-
two feet. The wall, which is four feet one inch at the bottom,
tapers down to about eight inches at the top. These figures
will give some idea of its size and enormous strength. It would
be much more interesting if anybody, I am not particular who,
knew when this and the other towers were built, and what they
were built for. There is, of course, a vast amount of specula-
tion in regard to their origin and use. One opinion is that
they were built by worshippers of the sun; another that they
were watch-towers (but the people of those times never put
watch-towers at the base of ridges unless they possessed a kind
of idiocy superior to anything this age knows of); still another,
that they were constructed as bell-towers. That they were for
protection is evident by the doors being so far from the ground
and there being no remnant of steps or stoops. A man who
had his door from ten to fifteen feet from the ground would
hardly be careless or indifferent in the building of a stoop.
There is as much divergence of opinion as to their age as to
their purpose. A claim has been put in to the effect that they
were built before the beginning of the Christian era, but I give no
encouragement to those people. I think they ought to be ar-
rested. I have tried to crowd in a theory that they are ancient
wells thrown up to the surface by some volcanic movement, and
roofed in the sharp conical form by an affrighted people, with a
view to turning them over and driving them into the earth again.
This is the most sensible idea on the subject that I have yet
heard. All that I need to make a sure thing of it is, to find
somebody who will explain. why they didn't do it. As that is
the easiest end of the argument, there ought to be no trouble in
finding *him*.

The owner of this land is a proud man. A round tower,
church, priory, stone coffin, oratory, graveyard, and pasturage

for forty cows, in one lump. A boy with red tops to his boots is in the slough of despond alongside of this chap.

When I got back to the boat I found the crew smoking a pipe, and the Pennsylvanian on the beach trying to get on a pair of tight boots over a pair of wet stockings. He had got one boot on, and had nearly conquered the other, but he had ruined that beach. In getting on the boots he had gone over a strip of ground about eighty feet in length and thirty feet in width, and had torn up the earth over every inch of it. When I came up he was as red in the face as a beet, and was yelling and stamping his foot in a perfect ecstacy of rage.

However, we soon fixed it, and put off for a continuation of the trip. The wind still held fair, and I took the helm, while the Pennsylvanian took a seat in the bow, and became immediately wrapt up in reflection.

IV.

A FAMOUS ISLAND.

WE passed several islands of no moment, and went by three or four farm-houses. The scenery was quiet and impressive. No life was seen on shore, and no sound came to us but the rippling of the water against the boat. There was a heavy bank of black clouds coming up above the horizon, but one could look upon it calmly, as this was an inland sheet of water, well protected by high ground.

We passed a high ridge and came out into an open and exposed part. Half-way across this the wind struck us with some considerable force, and the rain came down in torrents. The sail filled so rapidly as to cause the boat to career half-way over. It seemed as if a gale was tearing over the lake. The vessel rode on its edge, and I expected every moment we would upset and wet ourselves. I still hung to the helm and an umbrella, and kept to the upper side of the sloop. The crew hung to the sail with all his might, and the Pennsylvanian buried a face which had assumed the color of unbolted flour beneath the friendly cover of his umbrella.

All the while the storm increased in violence, and the boat was now riding in such a position that it was only by lapping my elbow over the taffrail that I kept myself from being spilled out. The crew wanted me to keep out at sea, but I concluded if I was to be wrecked, I would prefer being wrecked on land, and, which was of more importance, the umbrella was borrowed, and I did not want to lose it. So I run the barque for the first land, and we came upon the shore with a precision that was gratifying to me as a pilot, but with a force that very nearly dislocated the spine of the crew.

We got out of the boat as soon as possible, but it was not a hospitable shore. There were no trees but a small thorn growing out of the bank, and no shelter of any kind from the keen wind and driving rain. There we stood for three-quarters of an hour, keeping the tops of our heads perfectly dry with the umbrellas. If anybody could have observed us, he would have undoubtedly wondered where all the water came from which was running down our legs.

It was a pleasure party, and we were tourists, who had nothing to do but to travel around and enjoy ourselves, and live at hotels.

Several times I spoke to the Pennsylvanian about it, but he didn't seem to enter into the spirit of the remark.

He said if he could only get safely back to the Cumberland Mountains, he would never leave them for such an outlandish and cussed country as this.

I like to see a man show spirit.

The rain stopped, and we once more tried the boat. But we

didn't put up the sail. The Pennsylvanian said he would pull his arms out of their sockets first.

Our next point of interest was the island of Innismacsaint. There is a church ruin upon it; but it was a peculiar cross that I wanted to see. We reached there in about an hour. The cross was hardly worth the coming to see. It was rude in execution, and peculiar in construction, being of one piece, as if cut out of a rough slab. The boatman viewed the stone with considerable reverence.

" Is there anything remarkable about that?" I asked.

" Yes, sir. Every Easter morn, at the crowing of the cock, the cross jumps out oov the airth, and turns aroond thrice!"

" Will you be good enough to repeat that remarkable statement?" asked the Pennsylvanian, with breathless interest.

The crew complied.

" Did you ever see it perform that little exercise?"

The crew said he had not.

" Or anybody who has seen it?"

The crew shook his head.

" I wouldn't stand so close to it if I were you," said the Pennsylvanian, kindly; " it may jump out of the ground and kick you into the lake."

" Oh, it don't come out only at Easter," said the man, innocently.

" You can't always tell," said Penn. " This is just like Easter weather, and the cross may have mislaid its almanac."

The crew shook his head. The gentleman's excessive faith rather staggered him.

We got back to Enniskillen at dark, well tired, thoroughly wet, and two-thirds starved.

The next day was butter-market, and scores of country people were in town. Their counterparts can be seen in Castle Garden on the arrival of an emigrant ship. There was a large number of Connaught men, the pure Irish, so pure as not to have mastered the English language, who brought interpreters with them to enable them to make bargains with the village people. They wore corduroy pants, and long frieze coats, and decayed stovepipe hats. They are dying out, are the old Irish, and a new people are crowding them out. And the day will come when the pure Irish will have passed into history and legend.

Go up and down the principal streets of Belfast, Dublin, Cork, or any other Irish city, and four-fifths of the names on the places of business are not familiar as Irish names to us Americans.

And why not? Ireland is a fine country, has excellent seaports, good soil, and is most healthfully located. The Irish themselves are deserting it, and enterprising men of other countries are pushing in there. The result is as certain as the kick of a mule.

297

THE END OF A MONTH.

THE END OF A MONTH.

BY ALGERNON CHARLES SWINBURNE.

THE night last night was strange and shaken ;
    More strange the change of you and me.
Once more, the old love's love forsaken,
    We went out once more toward the sea.

For the old love's love-sake dead and buried,
    One last time, one more and no more,
We watched the waves set in, the serried
    Spears of the tide storming the shore.

Hardly we saw the high moon hanging,
    Heard hardly through the windy night
Far waters ringing, low reefs clanging,
    Under wan skies and waste white light.

With chafe and change of surges chiming,
    The clashing channels rocked and rang
Large music, wave to wild wave timing,
    And all the choral water sang.

Faint lights fell this way, that way floated,
    Quick sparks of sea-fire keen like eyes
From the rolled surf that flashed and noted
    Shores and faint cliffs and bays and skies.

The ghost of sea that shrank up sighing
    At the sand's edge, a short sad breath
Trembling to touch the goal, and dying
    With weak heart heaved up once in death —

301

THE END OF A MONTH.

The rustling sand and shingle shaken
   With light sweet touches and small sound —
These could not move us, could not waken
   Hearts to look forth, eyes to look round.

Silent we went an hour together,
   Under gray skies by waters white.
Our hearts were full of windy weather,
   Clouds and blown stars and broken light.

Full of cold clouds and moonbeams drifted
   And streaming storms and straying fires,
Our souls in us were stirred and shifted
   By doubts and dreams and foiled desires.

Across, aslant, a scudding sea-mew
   Swam, dipped and dropped, and grazed the sea ;
And one with me I could not dream you :
   And one with you I could not be.

As the white wing the white wave's fringes
   Touched and slid over and flashed past —
As a pale cloud a pale flame tinges
   From the moon's lowest light and last —

As a star feels the sun and falters,
   Touched to death by diviner eyes —
As on the old gods' untended altars
   The old fire of withered worship dies —

(Once only, once the shine relighted
   Sees the last fiery shadow shine,
Last shadow of flame and faith benighted,
   Sees falter and flutter and fail the shrine).

So once with fiery breath and flying
   Your winged heart touched mine and went,
And the swift spirits kissed, and sighing,
   Sundered and smiled and were content.

That only touch, that feeling only,
   Enough we found, we found too much ;
For the unlit shrine is hardly lonely
   As one the old fire forgets to touch.

THE END OF A MONTH.

Slight as the sea's sight of the sea-mew,
  Slight as the sun's sight of the star:
Enough to show one must not deem you
  For love's sake other than you are.

Who snares and tames with fear and danger
  A bright beast of a fiery kin,
Only to mar, only to change her
  Sleek supple soul and splendid skin?

Easy with blows to mar and maim her,
  Easy with bonds to bind and bruise;
What profit, if she yield her tamer
  The limbs to mar, the soul to lose?

Best leave or take the perfect creature,
  Take all she is or leave complete;
Transmute you will not form or feature,
  Change feet for wings or wings for feet.

Strange eyes, new limbs, can no man give her;
  Sweet is the sweet thing as it is.
No soul she hath, we see, to outlive her;
  Hath she for that no lips to kiss?

So may one read his weird, and reason,
  And with vain drugs assuage no pain;
For each man in his loving season
  Fools and is fooled of these in vain.

Charms that allay not any longing,
  Spells that appease not any grief,
Time brings us all by handfuls, wronging
  All hurts with nothing of relief.

Ah, too soon shot, the fool's bolt misses!
  What help? the world is full of loves;
Night after night of running kisses,
  Chirp after chirp of changing doves.

Should Love disown or disesteem you
  For loving one man more or less?
You could not tame your light white sea-mew,
  Nor I my sleek black pantheress.

THE END OF A MONTH.

For a new soul let whoso please pray,
　　We are what life made us, and shall be.
For you the jungle and me the sea-spray,
　　And south for you and north for me.

But this one broken foam-white feather
　　I throw you off the hither wing,
Splashed still with sea-scurf and salt weather,
　　This song for sleep to learn and sing —

Sing in your ear when, daytime over,
　　You, couched at long length on hot sand
With some sleek sun-discolored lover,
　　Wince from his breath as from a brand :

Till dreams of sharp gray north-sea weather
　　Fall faint upon your fiery sleep;
As on strange sands a strayed bird's feather
　　The wind may choose to lose or keep.

But I, who leave my queen of panthers,
　　As a tired honey-heavy bee
Gilt with sweet dust from gold-grained anthers
　　Leaves the rose-chalice, what for me ?

From the ardors of the chaliced centre,
　　From the amorous anther's golden grime,
That scorch and smutch all wings that enter,
　　I fly forth hot from honey-time.

But as to a bee's gilt thighs and winglets
　　The flower-dust and the flower-smell clings ;
As a snake's mobile rampant ringlets
　　Leave the sand marked with print of rings ;

So to my soul in surer fashion
　　Your savage stamp and savor hangs ;
The print and perfume of old passion,
　　The wild-beast mark of panther's fangs.

A COMMON STORY.

.

A Common Story.

BY MISS MULOCH.

" She loves with love that cannot tire;
  And if, ah woe! she loves alone,
Through passionate duty love flames higher,
  As grass grows taller round a stone."

— Coventry Patmore.

O, the truth's out. I'll grasp it like a snake —
It will not slay me. My heart shall not break
Awhile, if only for the children's sake.

For his too, somewhat. Let him stand unblamed;
None say, he gave me less than honor claimed,
Except — one trifle scarcely worth being named —

The *heart*. That's gone. The corrupt dead might be
As easily raised up, breathing — fair to see,
As he could bring his whole heart back to me.

I never sought him in coquettish sports,
Or courted him as silly maidens court,
And wonder when the longed-for prize falls short.

I only loved him — any woman would;
But shut my love up till he came and sued,
Then poured it o'er his dry life like a flood.

I was so happy I could make him blest!
So happy that I was his first and best,
As he mine — when he took me to his breast.

Ah me! if only then he had been true!
If for one little year, a month or two,
He had given me love for love, as was my due!

For he had told me, ere the deed was done,
He only raised me to his heart's dear throne —
Poor substitute! — because the queen was gone!

307

A COMMON STORY.

Oh, had he whispered, when his sweetest kiss
Was warm upon my mouth in fancied bliss,
He had kissed another woman like to this, —

It were less bitter! Sometimes I could weep
To be so cheated, like a child asleep —
Were not the anguish far too dry and deep.

So I built my house upon another's ground;
Mocked with a heart just caught at the rebound —
A cankering thing that looked so firm and sound.

And when that heart grew colder — colder still,
I, ignorant, tried all duties to-fulfil,
Blaming my foolish pain, exacting will,

All — anything but him. It was to be:
The full draught others drink up carelessly
Was made this bitter Tantalus-cup for me.

I say again — he gives me all I claimed,
I and my children never shall be shamed:
He is a just man — he will live unblamed.

Only — O God, O God! to cry for bread,
And get a stone! Daily to lay my head
Upon a bosom where the old love's dead!

Dead? — Fool! It never lived! It only stirred
Galvanic, like an hour-cold corpse. None heard:
So let me bury it without a word.

He'll keep that other woman from my sight.
I know not if her face be foul or bright;
I only know that it was his delight —

As his was mine: I only know he stands
Pale, at the touch of their long-severed hands,
Then to a flickering smile his lips commands,

Lest I should grieve, or jealous anger show.
He need not. When the ship's gone down, I trow,
We little reck whatever wind may blow.

A COMMON STORY.

And so my silent moan begins and ends,
No world's laugh or world's taunt, no pity of friends,
Or sneer of foes, with this my torment blends.

None knows — none heeds. I have a little pride;
Enough to stand up, wife-like, by his side,
With the same smile as when I was a bride.

And I shall take his children to my arms;
They will not miss these fading, worthless charms;
Their kiss — ah! unlike his — all pain disarms.

And haply, as the solemn years go by,
He will think sometimes, with regretful sigh,
The other woman was less true than I.

ONE-HORSE COLLEGES.

ONE-HORSE COLLEGES.

BY JAMES PARTON.

NOTHER college is announced. What a mania there is among rich men to found colleges! We have too many colleges already. In the single State of New York there are between thirty and forty institutions that call themselves colleges. In Ohio there are thirty or more, and the other States are plentifully provided. But in all the length and breadth of this land there is not one institution of learning which is thoroughly furnished for the work that fairly devolves upon a college in these times. This is so manifest that it has been seriously proposed to form a national society for the suppression of weak colleges, and adding the little strength they possess to institutions of some standing and efficiency.

In New England, for example, there are at least thirty colleges, among which there are three or four that are much superior to the rest in wealth, antiquity and reputation. What a prodigious gain it would be if the entire college force of the New England States could be concentrated upon the three or four strongest colleges! At once we could have true universities, equipped for the *increase* of knowledge, as well as for its diffusion.

At present our colleges do not and cannot do much for the advancement of knowledge, because nearly the whole strength of the professors is exhausted in mere teaching. In

313

a properly organized university the chief professor of each department would not have more than one hour's public duty to perform each day. His main strength would be spent in original investigation and experiment. One university in each of the States were far better than the hundreds of weak and struggling institutions that now pass round the hat.

We have not only too many colleges, but too many students in them. There are only two classes of young men that ought to go to college. One is the sons of men who are rich enough to maintain them in college, and for five years after graduation, while they are preparing for a learned profession. The other is young men of uncommonly gifted minds that passionately love knowledge, and cannot be content without pursuing it. For my part, I wish all the colleges would double or treble their rates of tuition, so as to keep out that great multitude of young men who have no right to be exempt from the ordinary labors of life. There is many a stout young fellow now being spoiled in college who ought to be at home helping "the old man" on the farm, or giving a lift to a laborious doctor or clergyman who is pinching all the family to provide his son with a college diploma.

It is a great delight and privilege to spend four years in acquiring knowledge. A villa at Newport is also a nice thing to have, and so is a two-hundred ton yacht. It may be a great pity that we cannot all have these pleasant things, but we *cannot*, and there is an end of it. Nearly every youth on earth, by the time he is eighteen years of age, ought to enter the college of life, and begin to acquire the art or business by which he means to live.

A youth that really and truly loves knowledge will get it, college or no college. I left school at eighteen or nineteen, just prepared to enter college, and began work at once, in a peculiarly absorbing and laborious vocation. By getting up very early in the morning I managed to study about an hour and a half a day, and on Sundays three hours. I kept up the practice for seven years, until I had read twice as much Latin and Greek, and nearly as much Mathematics, as I should have read in college.

You want knowledge, my boy? Get it. There it lies, ready for you. Don't sponge upon the old folks at home. One hour a day spent in judicious study, and kept up for fifty years, will put an intelligent person in possession of the substance of all the knowledge that exists.

Let us have no more "one-horse" colleges. If any rich man wants to do something useful in the college way, let him buy out a feeble college, settle pensions upon the aged professors, pull down the buildings, sell off the land, and thus peacefully extinguish the institution.

What we want in this country, above all things, is better and smaller primary schools, where the ceaseless tide of foreign ignorance that sets toward us, as well as the ignorance perpetuated at home, may be penetrated and enlightened. In this city of New York more than half of the children leave school forever before they are fourteen. The primary school is their only chance. The primary school is *our* only chance. And yet we are putting out the strength of the system in maintaining high schools and colleges.

We want colleges and universities, few in number, rich in the learning of their professors and in the character of their students. But as to the rudiments of knowledge, they should be as common, as free, and as inviting as air and water. A university can hardly be too large; a primary school can hardly be too small.

II

THE PHILOSOPHERS.

THE PHILOSOPHERS.

FROM SCHILLER.

BY GEORGE MACDONALD.

THE principle whence everything
   To life and shape ascended —
The pulley whereon Zeus the ring
Of Earth, which else in sherds would spring,
   Has carefully suspended —
To genius I yield him a claim
Who fathoms for me what its name,
   Save I withdraw its curtain :
   It is — ten is not thirteen.

That snow makes cold, that fire burns,
   That man on two feet goeth,
That in the heavens the sun sojourns —
This much the man who logic spurns
   Through his own senses knoweth ;
But metaphysics who has got
Knows that which scorches, freezes not ;
   Knows 'tis the moist that wetteth,
   And 'tis the rough that fretteth.

Great Homer sings his epic high ;
   The hero fronts his dangers ;
The brave his duty still doth ply —
And did it while, I won't deny,
   Philosophers were strangers :
If heart and brain have that achieved
Des Cartes and Locke had ne'er conceived —
   By these, as yet behooved,
   It possible was proved.

THE PHILOSOPHERS.

The strong man's right abideth still;
　The bold laughs like hyena;
Who rule not, servants' parts must fill;
It goes quite tolerably ill
　Upon this world's arena;
But how it would be if the plan
Of the universe now first began
　Is in their moral system,
　For all to read who list 'em.

"Man needs with man must linkèd be
　To reach the goal of growing;
In the whole only worketh he;
Many drops go to make the sea;
　Much water sets mills going.
Then with the wild wolves do not stand,
But knit the state's enduring band."
　From doctor's chair thus, tranquil
　Herr Pufendorf and swan-quill.

But since to all what doctors say
　Flies not as soon as spoken,
Nature will use her mother-way, —
See that her chain fly not in tway,
　The circle be not broken:
Meantime, until the world's great round
Philosophy in one hath bound,
　She keeps it on the move, sir,
　By hunger and by love, sir.

JOCK OF HAZELDEAN.

JOCK OF HAZELDEAN.

BY SIR WALTER SCOTT.

HY weep ye by the tide, ladie?
  Why weep ye by the tide?
I'll wed ye to my youngest son,
  And ye sall be his bride,
And ye sall be his bride, ladie,
  Sae comely to be seen "—
But aye she loot the tears down fa'
  For Jock of Hazeldean.

"Now let this wilfu' grief be done,
  And dry that cheek so pale;
Young Frank is chief of Errington,
  And lord of Langley-dale;
His step is first in peaceful ha',
  His sword in battle keen "—
But aye she loot the tears down fa'
  For Jock of Hazeldean.

"A chain of gold ye sall not lack,
  Nor braid to bind your hair;
Nor mettled hound, nor managed hawk,
  Nor palfrey fresh and fair;
And you, the foremost o' them a',
  Shall ride our forest queen "—
But aye she loot the tears down fa'
  For Jock of Hazeldean.

The kirk was decked at morning-tide,
  The tapers glimmered fair;
The priest and bridegroom wait the bride,
  And dame and knight are there.
They sought her baith by bower and lea,—
  The ladie was not seen,
She's o'er the Border, and awa'
  Wi' Jock of Hazeldean.

THE HIDDEN TREASURE.

THE HIDDEN TREASURE.

BY B. P. SHILLABER.

JOHN WENTWORTH, Royal Governor, the last
That in New Hampshire bore vice-regal sway,
Held court at Wolfeboro', by a lake, remote
From care of office, then made onerous
By the fierce restlessness of those he ruled,
Who caught the living spirit of the hour,
And threatened in the mood of discontent.
Portsmouth was turbulent, although respect
Checked violence 'gainst harm to genial John,
For all owned kindly fealty to him,
Although detesting his authority.
He was of Boston lineage and Harvard brand,
A generous, courtly, cultivated man,
Of tastes refined, with every wish awake
The people of his care to benefit.
Broad roads he builded and new ways devised
To give New Hampshire her predestined rank;
And Dartmouth felt the kindness of his heart
In many offices of generous care.
But "Royal Governor!" his title chafed
The temper of his people, and he flew
To this, his sylvan realm, for peace and rest.
He haply found it, did his buxom dame,
Widow of Atkinson, in ten days wed,
Post nubila at Atkinson's demise,
(What time, in going from the nuptial rites,
Did Arthur Brown, the rector, fall down stairs,
And, tributary to the season, break an arm),
Admit of peace domestic, breach of which
Were worse than din of direst politics.
His stately manse stood smiling by the shore,
A pile of goodly station, since destroyed
By fire which licked it to its cellar walls.

THE HIDDEN TREASURE.

Broad avenues connected with the road,
O'erarched by sturdy trees, while, back of all,
And far on every side, stretched hill o'er hill,
Giving incentive to the lively chase,
Where game abounded and adventure becked
The daring huntsman to his best essay.
A hospitable, cheerful home it was.
Amenities of old-time neighborhood
Existed thereabout without a check,
And one could scarcely dream the cloud suspent
So soon to merge the land in hostile flood!
'Twas spring-time, and the glory of the year
Was seen on verdant upland, vale, and mead;
The trees were rife with blossom, and the spray
Mellifluous with birds, while the green sod
Sparkled and glowed in jewelling of flowers.
Gay pleasure-boats went gliding o'er the lake,
Their white sails gleaming in the ruddy sun,
While from the teeming bosom of the wave
Were struggling drawn bright finny denizens,
To stir the taste with gustatory thrills —
When murmurs came, at first, of Lexington,
And the bold stand the yeomanry had made
'Gainst that prerogative which Wentworth held;
And then the full-toned clarion's fearful breath
Proclaiming that the hour of strife had come!
The land was rising, kingly rule was broke,
And gloomy eyes were bent on courtly John,
Though well content that he should e'er remain,
Could he of his commission be divest.
Then came the secret order to depart.
The Governor, too far from Barclay's ships,
Packed bag and baggage for a speedy flight.
The coach of state, rolled to the mansion door,
Hid by the night, received a weighty load:
Gay Lady Wentworth and the precious plate,
With its armorial bearings, and such cash
As then in argent sheen the coffers lined,
The Governor the last, who backed himself,
In stately silence, by my lady's side.
Mount quickly, coachman! footman, take your place!
On rolls the coach in cumbrous tardiness,

THE HIDDEN TREASURE.

And from the window Wentworth looks his last
On his broad acres, with a painful sigh,
While Lady Wentworth dreams of ball and rout
'Neath better auspices and loyal skies.
But heavy grew the way; the horses strove
And foamed with wearying effort to advance,
Until, quite failing, they no effort made.
The treasure must be left, or else the dame,
Its half-equivalent — forbid the thought! —
And there, beneath the solemn midnight stars,
The earth received in trust the precious store.
No more delay. The harborage was gained.
In Portsmouth, safe beneath the royal guns,
Did Wentworth tarry till rebellion took
Such sturdy presence that it was not safe
For royal governor to linger there;
And so he passed forever from the scene:
He ne'er regained the treasure hid in earth,
And no man knoweth whereabouts 'twas hid.
The path he went, traditional alone,
Affords no clue to its dark resting-place,
Though many seekers have essayed the task —
Running down through the century of years —
Of finding the so-much-desired prize.
And even now, at times, dim lights are seen
At night, when honest folks should be in bed,
Dancing about the meadow and the wood,
In hands of seekers for the buried pelf,
Led on by those who claim that they can see
Through all the mysteries of heaven and earth.
The earth is honeycombed with punctures made
By prodding iron bars; but over all
A monumental disappointment reigns.
Perhaps John Wentworth guards the spot himself,
Not yet selected his adopted heir.

POOR JAMES WYMPER.

POOR JAMES WYMPER.

BY ALBANY FONBLANQUE,

Author of " The Tangled Skein," etc.

HEN he was a child they called him " poor little James." He wasn't little, and he wasn't poor, so far as worldly goods went; nor did those who called him " poor " use the word in kindness toward the motherless, neglected boy. He had red eyelids. No power could brush his hair smooth, or keep the knees of his trousers clean. He had a wonderful faculty for cutting his fingers, and wrapping them up in unpleasant-looking rags. He always had a cold in his head. At the age of twelve he could barely read two syllables. His only use in the world appeared to be to serve as an awful example to naughty boys, who would play with knives and disliked soap and water; and for this purpose he was used pretty freely. They sent him to a big school, where he did nothing but get bullied; and when his father died, and left him very poor in a new sense of the word, the distant relative who took him in charge out of charity could find no better employment for him than to sweep out the office and run of errands. By this time he had ceased to be " poor little James," and became POOR JAMES WYMPER.

He could do nothing good of himself, and by some curious perversity set himself to undo the good that others had done. He had a craze for taking things to pieces by no means equalled by his capacity to put them together again. He complained that they did not give him time, and declared that this granted, the condition of the victims of his handiwork would be improved. Be this as it might be, every piece of mechanism that fell in his way, from his cousin's sewing-machine to the great hydraulic press at his protector's works, was made to suffer.

He had a fatal aptitude for being always in the way. He seemed to be all elbows. He could not move ten steps to save his life without treading upon some one's toes, or upsetting something. When you spoke to him, he was always in a fog. "The boy is half an idiot," groaned the worthy cotton-spinner, whose bread he ate.

At the age of eighteen he had made but two friends in the world, a blacksmith and a cat—an evil-minded black Tom, who swore at every one else, and bit them savagely when they attempted to put him through the tricks which poor James Wymper had taught him. Amateur hammering at the forge did not improve untidy Jim's appearance, and his cat — not being in a show — did not increase his income. He ran errands for his cousin like a boy when he had attained man's estate, until one day when he ran one for himself — and did not come back again.

Fears were entertained that he had come to a bad end. The police were put in motion and rewards offered; but his friend the blacksmith, upon being pressed, said that he had gone to "Mereker"—cat and all.

I do not think that his relations were broken-hearted. I fancy that good Mr. Bryce, the cotton-spinner, was rather glad to be rid of his wife's cousin, the errand-boy. His wife, who was not unkind to the forlorn lad in a way of her own,— a very cold way it was,— sighed several times apropos of nothing, and murmured, "Poor James Wymper!"

Five years passed, and Mrs. Bryce was left a widow, by no

means so well provided for as she. expected to be. Moreover there was a lawsuit about the will, and a squabble in the winding-up of the partnership. She was glad to " get shut " — as her defunct lord would have said — of Manchester ; and seeing an advertisement to the effect that a widow lady, having a house too large for her, pleasantly situated on the Thames near Maidenhead, was prepared to share it with just such a person as herself, transported herself thither, after a due exchange of references and such-like formalities, and found no reason to regret what she had done.

The other widow does not figure much in this story, and therefore it will be enough to say that she was a quiet, lady-like woman, rather afraid of her partner in house-keeping, with a daughter, aged eighteen, who ruled the pair, and made the place very pleasant.

Bessy Jervoice was not pretty. Besides her eyes she had not a good feature in her face ; but it was a *good* face — earnest and loving, with a sub-current of fun running under it (as the stream runs under the water-lilies), and rippling out constantly. Her figure and her hair were simply perfection. Her little thoroughbred hands were ever busy, and the patter of her dainty feet was pleasant music in many a poor cottage.

Things went on very smoothly at the river-side villa until one rainy day, when, without a " with your leave," or " by your leave," or letter, or telegram, or message, or any other sort of preparation, in marches poor James Wymper, dripping with rain and splashed with mud up to his hat !

" If you please, cousin Margaret, I've come back," he said, subsiding in his old, low-spirited way into an amber-satin drawing-room chair, which in two minutes he soaked through and through.

That was all. No excuse, no petition ; a simple announcement that he had come back, conveyed in a manner which made it sufficiently clear that he intended to remain. "If you please, cousin Margaret, I've come back." Not another word did he say, and relapsed into thinking of something else, as usual.

Interrogated respecting his luggage, he replied that it was on the hall-table, and there, sure enough, was found a sodden bundle, containing a soiled flannel-shirt, a pair of slippers, two pipes, a cloth cap without a peak, and a sailor's knife. In answer to further inquiries he stated that his means were eightpence, that he had been living in America, that he had walked from Liverpool, and that he wanted something to eat. When dried and fed, and asked what he was going to do, he said, "Whatever you please;" and appearing to consider that all difficulty was thus disposed of, he went to sleep.

Poor Mrs. Bryce was at her wits' end. Ordinary hints were thrown away upon such a man. When she said she supposed he was going on to London, he replied, Oh, dear no, he had come from London. When she told him she was only a lodger in the house, he observed that it was a very nice house to lodge in. I have said that she was kind to him in her way when he was an errand-boy, and somehow she could not be hard upon him now. There was something half ludicrous, half melancholy, in his helplessness that disarmed them all. Bessy declared him to be the largest baby she had ever seen, persisted in speaking of him as *it*, and scandalized the matrons by inquiring gravely after tea which of them was going to put *it* to bed.

"It's rather unkind for you to jest so, Bessy," said poor Mrs. Bryce, "when you see how distressed I am. What on earth am I to do?"

"I suppose it's too old for the Foundling?" mused Bessy.

"Bessy, be quiet!" said her mother.

"You dear old darling," said the pert one afterwards, "don't you see that *we* cannot treat this thing seriously without making

it doubly painful for dear Mrs. Bryce? It will all come right
in the end."

"Yes, my dear, but when is the end to begin?"

It was to begin by special arrangement the next day, after
breakfast; when the following conversation took place:—

"Now, James," said his cousin, "we shall not be interrupted
for some time, and you must really give me your serious
attention."

"Yes, cousin Margaret."

"You see, James, you are a man now, and must act and be
treated — do you understand? — *treated*, like other people."

"That's just what I want to be."

"Well, then, I must tell you frankly that I am much annoyed
by your coming here as you did."

"It wasn't my fault that it rained, cousin Margaret. I wish
it hadn't," he replied piteously.

"I'm not speaking of your coming in wet and spoiling the
chairs, sir; I am much annoyed at your coming here at all."

The good widow thought that she would get on best by being
angry, but it was no use.

"Where else was I to go to?" he asked.

"How you found me out, I cannot think," sighed the victim.
The observation was an unlucky one.

"Ah, ha!" he chuckled, "you thought I was a stupid, did
you?"

And then followed a long, weary story of how, passing through
Manchester, he had seen this person and spoken to that, and
obtained the clue by which he had hunted his listener down.
What made it more provoking was the credit he took for this
cleverness. He warmed to his subject as he went on, and fin
ished with the air of a man who had rendered an important
service, and expected to have it promptly recognized.

This threw his victim's cut-and-dried speeches off the line.

337

" Oh, dear, oh, dear!" she cried. " It doesn't matter how you found me out; you *have* done so. The question is, what am I to do with you, now you're here? What *am* I to do with you?"

" I don't know, cousin Margaret."

" You don't know! A pretty answer for a man of five-or-six-and-twenty. Now look here, James Wymper. I should like to do something for you for your poor mother's sake, but I cannot; and — and you have no *right* to thrust yourself upon me like this, and — and — are you attending to me, James Wymper?"

" Yes, cousin Margaret," he replied with a jerk, coming suddenly out of his fog.

" What was I saying?"

" That you would like to do something for me for my poor mother's sake."

" That was only half what I said, sir. How dare you pick out my words like that! I went on to say that I couldn't do anything for you, and I can't. I've not the means. I'm very poor; I can hardly manage for myself. My husband left me very badly off."

" Did he leave me anything?"

" You! after your conduct — running away, and frightening us as you did! Is it likely?"

" I know it was wrong to run away, cousin Margaret, but you see I've come back again," he said with the utmost gravity.

This was conclusive. For the last half-hour she had been trying to din into his head that he had no business to come back, and here he was, taking credit for having returned, as an act which was to cancel all the offences of his youth! Perceiving that his reply had troubled her, he proceeded to promise upon his word of honor that he would never, *never* run away again What was to be done with such a man? Talking was

338

clearly useless. One of two courses only remained — to endure him, or call a policeman and turn him out neck and crop.

Mrs. Bryce did not call a policeman.

The conduct of poor James Wymper during the next two or three days was what, in another man, would have roused the indignation of all concerned by its almost sublime audacity. The proceedings of Mr. Charles Mathews in *Cool as a Cucumber* are timid and retiring in comparison with those of Mrs. Jervoice's unwelcome guest. If the house and all it contained had belonged to him, and its inhabitants were dependents upon his bounty, he could not have behaved more freely; and all this with an air of innocence which utterly disarmed opposition.

"Oh, never mind me," was his refrain; "I don't want to trouble anybody. I'll do it all for myself. *I'm* all right. You let me alone and see."

His first great exploit was to precipitate himself upon a washing and wringing machine which he found, out of order and disused, in a cellar; and whether he had improved in dexterity, or sufficient time was granted him for the realization of his ideas, need not be discussed here. The result was satisfactory. Not only did he put the thing into working order, but he worked it himself, to the intense delight of Bessy and consternation of the cook.

Many other useful things he did. He made a wind-mill which pumped water up to the top of the house, and saved the sixpence a day which had been paid to a boy for this labor. He mended an old boat that there was, and took Bessy out for rows on the river. He became that young lady's right-hand man in her garden. Before a month was over, not only had cousin Margaret become quite resigned to have him on her hands, but Mrs. Jervoice refused to accept any remuneration for his board and lodging, declaring that he was well worth his keep. It was something, you see, for these lone women to have a man about the house who could and would put his hand to this and that. He did not cut his fingers now.

Before this satisfactory condition of affairs had been arrived at, tailor and hosier had been set to work, and really poor James Wymper brightened up wonderfully in appearance under their hands. If his head had not been so big, and his elbows and knees so uncomfortably conspicuous, he would not have been a bad-looking man. He was evidently a good-hearted one. He would do anything in his power, poor fellow, for any one; was in fact rather too active sometimes when he had been longer than usual in one of his fogs, on which occasions he would labor like an amiable bull in a china shop, and cause some consternation. Of course he made friends with the nearest blacksmith.

In the early days, when he had not ceased to be considered a nuisance and an intruder, Bessy had stood his friend. One always takes an interest in those one befriends, and Bessy took a great interest in poor James Wymper — drawing him out, encouraging him, and defending him against practical jokes; but as time passed, this young person's feelings towards him appeared to undergo a change. Instead of praising what he did, and encouraging him to farther exertion, she found fault and snubbed him. She ceased to make fun of him as "it," and had a store of little bitter, disparaging remarks — about his dependence, his want of self-respect, and so on — ready to shoot at him. "I think you are too severe on poor James Wymper," Mrs. Jervoice would say; "he is really very willing, and one must not expect too much of him, poor fellow!" If another man had done what he did, he would not have been damned with such faint praise, but he was only "poor James Wymper;" and, like the proverbial prophet, had little credit in his own country.

One morning was marked with an unusual event — poor

James Wymper received a letter with American stamps upon
it.

Amongst the visitors at Willow Bank — the Thames-side
villa of Mrs. Jervoice — was a certain Mr. Augustus Bailey, a
young gentleman of pleasing and varied accomplishments. He
could sing you music-hall songs nearly as well as the "great
comiques" his masters. He could imitate most celebrated
actors, and was a mighty punster. For the better exhibition of
such talents a butt was indispensable, and he found one ready
made in poor James Wymper. It is needless to observe that
poor James Wymper did not love Mr. Augustus Bailey; but it
was curious that a usually amiable girl like Bessy Jervoice should
encourage the latter in sallies which were often as ungenerous
as they were insolent.

" I want you to put my sewing-machine in good order, Mr.
Wymper," said Bessy one day, "and mind it works smoothly, for
I've got to make a dress in a hurry."

" What for?" asked he.

" A picnic."

" What's a picnic?"

" Don't tease."

" Very well;" and he set to work on the sewing-machine.

Bessy took a seat beside him, and, mollified by his obedience,
condescended to explain the rites and mysteries of a picnic.
This one was got up by Mr. Augustus Bailey, and — as she narrated — it was "Mr. Bailey will provide" this, and "Mr. Bailey
thinks" that; until the workman threw down his screw-driver in
a passion, and exclaimed, "Confound Mr. Bailey!" Bessy was
astonished. She got as far as, "Why, you're not jeal —" when
she became very red, and checked herself.

" I'm not what?" asked poor James Wymper.

" You're not so stupid as you try to make out, sir."

" That's not what you were going to say."

"How do you know?"

"You said, 'you are not jel'—something."

"Not jelly then, or salt or sugar, that you should melt in a shower," she replied. The last-quoted opinion of the great Augustus had been that it was sure to rain, and so this observation of Miss Bessy was not as inappropriate as it may at first appear. But why should she have blushed so? And if she had really intended to tell him he was not jelly, why did she not go on and say so? Besides, he had not confounded Mr. Bailey, because that authority had predicted rain, and Miss Bessy knew it. She flattered herself that she had got very cleverly out of a difficulty, and the blush changed to a smile; but she had only made bad worse. To tell a man that he will not suffer under the rain on a stated occasion naturally implies that he may be subjected to a wetting on such occasion; and—

"Oh, then I'm to go!" said poor James.

This was a poser. He had not been invited, and there was a reason why he could not be. He looked up from his work with such a happy smile on his great, broad face that Bessy's heart smote her.

"Well, you see, the gentlemen are mostly friends of Mr. Bailey. We invite them, you know, but—you won't be hurt if I tell you the truth, James Wymper?"

"Does truth hurt?"

"Sometimes. The fact is, that it is customary at water picnics for the gentlemen to provide the boats and music and wine, and that costs money, you know."

"Oh, so I cannot go because I have not got money to pay my share, eh?"

"You would not like to place yourself under an obligation to Mr. Bailey and his friends, I suppose?" she said with a sneer.

"I wish you would not curl your lip so when you speak, Miss

Jervoice. That *does* hurt," he said, with a low voice and bended head.

" I beg your pardon ! "

" Oh, never mind. But suppose," he continued gaily, as though a bright thought had struck him, " I were to help to row one of the boats, and arrange the dinner and that, wouldn't they let me come ? "

" I never saw such a man ! " Bessy exclaimed, losing all patience. " Have you no single spark of self-respect — no dignity ? Oh, how can you be so mean-spirited ! "

" Work is as good as money any day," he replied, looking her full in the face.

" Yes, if you go as a servant."

" You said just now that every one had to make himself useful at a picnic."

" It's no use arguing with you; you *will* not or cannot understand."

" You don't want me to go ? "

" On the contrary, I should like you to join us, if — "

" If I had the money ? "

" If you could go on an equality with the rest."

" Well, I've got five pounds. Is that enough ? "

" Five times enough. But where on earth did you get it ? "

" Sam sent it in that letter."

" And who is ' Sam,' pray ? "

" My chum in Chicago."

" Don't you think it would be more proper to give the money to your cousin, who has been so liberal to you ? "

" Oh, I'll pay her some day. This runs first-rate now," he said, collecting his tools. " Do let me go to the picnic. Come, now, you help me to get an invitation, and I'll make your skirt."

And, if you'll believe me, this man set to work with the machine he had just set in order, and ran seven breadths of the blue silk together as tight as wax and as straight as a rule, without missing a stitch.

As Bessy made a point of his being invited, and Mr. Augustus Bailey was her humble servant, and hoped to be something more, no difficulty arose on this point; but on another there was trouble. Some Cockneys had misbehaved themselves on the meadows where it was fixed that our party should dine, and the proprietor, hardening his heart against all picknickers, had refused his permission. The outing was nearly given up, when it was discovered that a mile or two farther on there was an estate to let bordering on the river, and the great Augustus made it all right with the agent.

The next day poor James Wymper disappeared before breakfast, and did not return till night.

Where had he been? To London. What for? Why, to buy some new clothes, to be sure! Did they think he was going to let that skunk (by which term, I am sorry to say, he permitted himself to designate the elegant and highly-scented Augustus Bailey) — did they think he was going to let that skunk insult him again about his coat?

"I hope you did not think I had run away again, cousin Margaret," he added with some anxiety,

There was nothing to find fault with in his personal appearance on the morning of the picnic — dark green and black heather mixture suit, tie to match, black felt wideawake, with a little mallard's feather stuck in the band.

"Dear me!" exclaimed Mrs. Jervoice; "he looks quite handsome!"

"Who is that talking to Mrs. Bryce?" asked the inevitable curate. "What a magnificent head he has!"

"*Wh—at!*" shouted the great Augustus.

"Magnificent to a phrenologist, I mean," the curate explained.

" Ha, ha, ha ! " roared the " skunk." " Look here, you fellow; here's a joke ! Mr. Day says he is a phrenologist, and finds Wymper's head *magnificent !* Ha, ha, ha ! Why, don't you know," he added in a whisper, " that the fellow's half an idiot ? "

During the embarcation and the row up the river poor James Wymper's conduct was peculiar. Instead of doing everything for everybody, as usual, he stood apart, and ordered people about royally.

" I'm quite pleased with you to-day," whispered Bessy, as he handed her out of the boat on the banks of the estate that was *to let.*

" Now, I say, you — er — what's your name ? — you, Wymper, come and help take the hampers out ! " said the great Augustus.

" Take them out yourself, you — er, Bailey ! " he shouted back. " You haven't been rowing ; I have ; " and he strutted on to join a party of ladies, including Bessy. Bessy turned on hearing the loud talking, and somehow got detached from her friends.

" Why are you pleased with me to-day, Miss Jervoice ? " he asked as they sauntered on together side by side through the shrubbery.

" Would you very much like to know ? "

" I shouldn't have asked unless."

" Guess then."

" Because I've been making myself disagreeable ? "

" I don't think you have been making yourself disagreeable."

" Well, then, because I haven't been making myself useful ? "

" That is not the way to put it ; but you are burning."

" Because I've got new clothes ? "

" Nonsense ! you know what I mean, or you wouldn't have answered as you did at first. Good gracious ! I hope it is not going to rain."

" Tell me why," he persisted.

" Oh, don't tease."

" All right."

As soon as he did not want to know, she, woman-like, wanted to tell him. So in a minute or two she began again.

" It is a great mistake to make one's self too cheap. There are some people who gain respect by being good-natured, and some people who lose it."

" Ah, I see ! " he replied ; " I won't be good-natured any more."

" Oh, you *are* so silly ! Don't you know there is a medium in everything? But really it *is* going to rain; I felt a big drop. My new blue costume will be ruined."

" Well, we can go into the house. Here it is."

The shrubbery walk was so thickly hedged that they had not seen where they were going, and at a sudden turn there, sure enough, was the villa close at hand.

" I suppose we might stand under the veranda?" suggested Bessy; and, doubling up her skirts, she ran for it; for the rain came down with a dash — came down with a slant, too, driven by the wind, so that the veranda gave them little shelter.

" I wonder if any of the windows " (they were French windows, opening to the ground) " are open?" said her companion, trying them.

" Oh, we mustn't go in," said Bessy.

" Very well."

" But the splashing is spoiling my dress; don't you see? and my boots will be wet through," pleaded the inconsistent one.

" Then go in," said poor James Wymper, opening a window, " and I will run round and make it all right with the people in charge."

In ten minutes he rejoined her, saying that it *was* all right.

" What a pretty room ! " she said, looking at herself in the pier-glass. (Did you ever know a girl to enter a strange room without going straight up to the glass?)

" Hum — m, yes," he replied ; " but the fellow who built it was an ass. Why, you have to twist your neck to get a view of the river from these things " — with a contemptuous kick towards the French windows. " If I had it, I'd knock that veranda into a cocked hat, break out a big bow in the middle, and then it would be something like."

" Oh, you'd work wonders, I dare say," she said, rather crossly ; " only it would be as well to do something towards getting a house of your own before you think about improving other people's."

" It *would* be nice to have a house of one's own," he said, " particularly — "

" Well, go on."

" Particularly if it had a bow window."

" James Wymper ! "

" And a pretty meadow for picnics ; but I suppose it would not do to give people leave to picnic on one's grounds ? "

" Why not ? "

" Would that not be being good-natured ? "

" I did not mean that sort of good nature."

" If I had a fine house and grounds like this, I might be good-natured then ? "

" It's no use arguing with you," she replied sharply. " Is it ever going to leave off? Our picnic will be quite spoiled."

" Never mind ; we'll have another, soon. I dare say Sam will send me some more money."

" Are you not ashamed of yourself, James Wymper, to take money like a beggar ? " she said, with flashing eyes.

" Oh, I don't take it like a beggar."

" Yes, you do."

" No, I don't."

" A man who takes money that he does not earn, takes it like a beggar — there ! "

"Who told you I take money I do not earn?"

"Of course you cannot earn it."

"Why, of course?"

"What a plague you are! What do you do to earn it?"

"Nothing now."

"What have you ever done?"

"Lots of things."

"Do you mean to say that this person you call 'Sam' really owes you money?" She came quickly to his side as she spoke, and laid her hand on his arm.

"Yes, he does."

"What for?"

"For my share of what we did at Chicago."

"That could not have been much."

"What?"

"Your share."

"Sam says it was half: Sam's generally right."

"Where is Chicago?"

"Well, now, that is good! You don't know where Chicago is, and you're clever. *I* know."

"Of course, when you've been there."

"That's true," he replied, after reflection.

"Did you really get your living there?" she asked.

"Yes, I did."

"Then go back. O James, do — *do* go back. I can't bear to see you as you are — dependent and looked down on. Oh, do go back, and work like a man. I suppose it is because we women are so dependent that we prize and honor independence. For me there is nothing so contemptible as a strong man who is idle and contented. Go back to Chicago. I shall be sorry to lose you, because — because I like you very much, and you have been very kind to me; but, don't you know, cannot you imagine, how happy, how glorious it must be to strive and conquer; to stand erect before the world, owing nothing but to God and your own honest labor?"

"I can, I do!" he cried, starting up. "It *is* glorious. Do *you* know, can you imagine, what it is to have people despising you as a fool — an incapable — and yet to feel here (he struck his massive forehead as he spoke) that you are wronged, that you had not fair play? To feel knowledge, invention, power, coming, growing, *burning* in your brain; — to see the ideas thus born forming themselves under your hands, and to KNOW that they were right and sound; — to make those who came to scoff, stay to praise? For this," he added, in a lower voice, "I humbly thank Almighty God, and good Sam Thacker!"

Now, when Bessy Jervoice had had her say, as above recorded, and, piqued by surprise and excitement, and perhaps by something else, had said more than a well-regulated young lady ought to say, she naturally sat down and cried; but wonderstruck by the response she had evoked — a response which grew more astonishing, more fervid as it proceeded — she slowly raised her eyes; and there, before her, stood a James Wymper she had never seen before. Not a *poor* James Wymper in any sense of the term. The curate was right; and the magnificent head, its features lit up with pride and — well, it must out — *love*, was a sight to see.

"Forgive me," he said, taking her trembling hand, "for having played a part. It was Sam Thacker's doing. Said Sam, 'You go back a rich man amongst those cusses' (Sam is a regular Yankee, you know), 'and they'll just crawl over you, and suck your vitals; you sham poor and stupid, and you'll soon see who's who.' Ah, Bessy, how kind you were to me at first! Am I wrong in thinking, in hoping, that what was not so kind lately was meant for my good?"

"Oh, but how unfair — how —"

"Scold me presently, but hear my story. I ran away from

Manchester, because I felt dimly that I could improve and invent things if I had a chance; but I was awkward with my hands. I could not draw, I could not plan. I was not ready with my tongue; I could not explain; I got impatient when people did not understand me, and all went badly until I fell in with Sam. Sam is the handiest fellow in the world; and as for talking, he could coax a 'possum out of his hole; but, at first, he hadn't one idea of his own. Well, we worked together, and as we went on, I got handy and Sam inventive; and to make a long story short, we sold two patents for fifty thousand dollars each, and we have four more, which bring in about two thousand a year in English money as royalties. I'm going to pay my share in this picnic out of that money; and it is quite true that Sam sent me the cash, because all my remittances come through him."

"I — I think," stammered astonished Bessy, "that we must not stop here any longer."

"Just a few minutes."

"They will think it so odd."

"As you please. Will you have these flowers?" And he took a bouquet from a vase on the table.

"Put them back directly. How can you! Taking what does not belong to you! O James!"

"I bought the estate last week," replied poor James Wymper quietly, "and I suppose the flowers go with it."

"Mr. Wymper, are you mad, or am I dreaming?" gasped Bessy.

"I bought the place as soon as I heard you were coming here. That's why I went to London — and to get some clothes."

"Please take me back to mamma;" and Bessy began to cry again.

"When you have answered me one question. I hardly dar. ask it; but yet — "

But yet! The stupid fellow! it was evident that he had not yet patented a machine for divining a girl's thoughts. He hem'd and stammered and beat about the bush, as he did in his pre-Sam-Thacker days, and at last got it out. What was it?

Bessy left that room, as Sam would say, "inside an elbow," with an accepted lover's kiss tingling her lips, and glorifying her heart.

Never mind what has become of the picknickers; never mind the astonishment of Mr. Augustus Bailey and the rest when, invited by the master of the house to have their dance in his dining-room (on account of the wet), they learned who that master was; never mind the explanation with cousin Margaret. The only thing which I regret not having space to do justice to is the conduct of Sam at the wedding, and the burning wrath and indignation of the honest fellow when he heard that his partner had been known as POOR JAMES WYMPER.

"*Poor!*" he almost howled; "why, there aint a *ma*chine running on this old hemisphere, or in the *U*nited States, that he can't *im*prove and beat. *Poor!* and he with the heart of a child and the brain of a Newton! *Poor* indeed! Let me catch any one calling him *poor*, and I'll get mad; and when I get mad, there's shootin' round. Yes, *sir.*"

TWO LIVES.

Two Lives.

BY EUGENE MONTGOMMERY.

I.

THEY watched the sun droop sadly through the west,
As droop the souls of men to dreamy rest;
Blood-red and golden, as it sank away
Life seemed to grow more faint, then softly die;
Gray shadows lay across the trembling sky,
And night sat weeping for the day.

II.

But as they looked, a long, thin streak of light
Stretched far beyond the portals of the night,
Like some red phantom of unearthly dream,
Darting its tongues of flame on worlds around.
How wonderful! Is there no power to bound
The things that are, the things that seem?

III.

Who hath not felt the mystery to come,
The thought eternal, once so vague and dumb,
Whilst gazing mute upon the rage of Hell,
Mingled with Heaven's sweet love and purity?
And is the sky not Heaven's infinity
Where reigns the God whom men repel?

IV.

A boy and girl, two breathing souls of chance,
Two marks of life, two creatures of a trance!
They watched the sky — who knoweth what they saw?
Perchance 'twere better they had never been,
They seem too pure for man's proud world of sin,
So full of innocence and awe!

355

V.

The boy lay silent on the shadowy grass,
Watching the light, as all bright visions, pass;
   Watching it steal across the girl's sweet face,
Into her eyes, where burned a strange wild fire,
Into her flowing hair, — then higher, higher,
   Till gloom enshrouded every grace.

VI.

He sighed; and, as he sighed, the rustling breeze
Wearily chanted through the forest trees;
   The whole dark earth seem rocking to and fro;
The distant river broke with gasps of pain
Upon the heavy shore, where long had lain
   The memories of unbroken woe.

VII.

But what was darkness to his eager eyes?
Her face he knew more wondrous than the skies.
   He knew each quiver of the strong, full mouth,
Each queenly movement of the slender head,
Her sweet, odd smile, which seemed in secret wed
   To some weird fancy of the South.

VIII.

And what was woe to them, and what was thought?
Ah! ye may ask, but there are natures wrought
   In all the fulness of reality:
Young hearts whose yearnings are the worlds they feel,
Young hearts from which the years will never steal
   The sense sublime of what they see.

IX.

Oft did they wander in the twilight's haze,
Drinking the sweetness of the passing days;
   Living together, mingling smiles and tears,
Telling of hopes that men so rarely tell,
Dreaming the dreams that lives so soon dispel,
   Dreaming beyond the silent years.

X.

To-night with thoughtful mien they softly sit,
Whilst weird, gray shadows round them dimly flit:
  Two babes of nature wrapped in one great soul,
They seem the relics of a world gone by,
A world whose meaning men in vain deny,
  A world of hearts', life's, broken goal.

XI.

The boy arises suddenly and cries:
"Behold the moon, sweet Pearl, — behold the skies
  Bathing their features in her golden light.
Oh, would that we could sit forever thus,
Free, free as are the birds that sing for us!
  Ah, bright, bright days, why seek ye flight?

XII.

"To-night, sweet Pearl, the moon seems fair to me,
Fairer, I deem, than aught of land or sea;
  I seem to watch my eyes in her great face,
So pale and sad, as is the face of death.
Why do we live, sweet Pearl? Is life a breath
  Of something that we love to chase?

XIII.

"I know not what the world is, but I fear
'Tis full of sadness. Do not men appear
  To look with sorrow on our fair green land?
I know not what it is, but I have thought,
And I have found perhaps what God has taught,
  What even a child can understand.

XIV.

"I know not what the world is. Shall I know?
Why should I, Pearl, if all is strife and woe?
  Are we not happy thus, alone and free,
Alone and happy, living as the flowers?
Will God destroy the beauty that is ours
  If we remain as we should be?

XV.

"Do I not feel, and doth the moon not feel?
Do we not live for those sweet loves that steal
  To our dear hearts as angels to the sky?
What mean the loud, wild curses of the town?
What means the wearing of a golden crown?
  What are the gems that men would buy?"

XVI.

The girl looks up: she is no infant now;
Rather some spirit round whose pallid brow
  Are weaved the tresses of eternity.
Her great black eyes, aglow with brimming tears,
Flash out the thoughts that dwell more deep than years,
  Within the soul's infinity.

XVII.

"Alas!" she murmured, "I have felt before,
As thou, dear Harold, what will be no more.
  Yet I was happy, — I, a fair, young child;
I asked not why, since God had made me so;
I loved all things, for all seemed born to show
  The heart can never be defiled.

XVIII.

"How bright the days have been for thee and me!
Could we two live apart? No, no! for see,
  There is no hope once mine that is not thine.
Yet we must part — alas! forever part,
The world cares naught for us, and life's poor heart
  With ours and Death will intertwine.

XIX.

"Didst thou not watch the sky whilst flames of fire
Reddened the wide, low west? 'Twas fate's desire
  Thus to reveal what life doth ne'er reveal.
How sad, sad, sad seemed all the weeping trees!
How sad, sad, sad life's hopes and sympathies!
  How deep the pain that naught can heal!

358

TWO LIVES.

XX.

"For lo! I saw a woman, tall and fair,
Brushing the diamonds from her golden hair,
  Bathing within the sun's soft, mellowing rays.
She smiled at me, and I smiled back at her;
I would have bowed me as her worshipper,
  But she forbade me with a gaze.

XXI.

"Ah me! she smiled not long, for when the sun
Lay trembling like a heart whose work is done,
  I saw her turn and fall upon her knees,
Beating her breast, from which the warm blood flowed,
Tearing her soft, bright hair, as though endowed
  With rage more awful than the seas.

XXII.

"All soon was dark; yet through the wide still gloom,
I heard a voice, the cold, low voice of doom:
  Sadly it echoed through the ghostly air,
Sadly it came and trembled overhead,
Moaning of love, but of a love long dead,
  Moaning of all the soul's despair.

XXIII.

"Ah! Harold, I shall die, — for this was Death;
I felt upon my cheeks his icy breath;
  I felt his hands upon my heart, whilst low
He murmured words that make me tremble still.
Ah! Harold, I shall die; for lives fulfil
  What souls to souls so plainly show.

XXIV.

"Yes, I shall die; and will the sweet birds sing,
And will the flowers smile at their blossoming,
  And will the breezes warble to the stream,
When I am laid where hearts so long to sleep?
Ah! I could quit them all, and never weep,
  If thou couldst share my last long dream."

TWO LIVES.

XXV.

"Sweet Pearl!" he answers sadly, "thou shalt live:
The long bright hours to thee will gladly give
  What Death can trouble not, nor sorrow share;
Thy love is mine, and thou must live for me,
And thou must laugh again, for, darling, see
  The moon smiles gaily through the air.

XXVI.

"Chase from thy heart the load that night hath brought.
Ah! wouldst thou die? No, Death is never sought:
  Thou hast but dreamed. What can the sky foretell?
The wide, wide world hath many a song for thee,
And many a work, and many a hope for me;
  Our loves will doubt forever quell."

XXVII.

The girl looked up, and lightly tossed her head;
Then, like a sunbeam, towards the village sped,
  Flinging her tresses in the moon's pale smile:
Was this the child whose soul had vaguely told
Of life unspoken, fate that years unfold,
  And death, whose teachings men revile?

*   *   *   *   *   *

XXVIII.

The sun once more lay golden in his shrouds;
The long red light streamed ghost-like through the clouds,
  Falling like drops of blood upon two graves,
Two small, sad graves, that stretched like autumn leaves
Upon the face of Earth. Ah! Pearl, who grieves
  That hearts are swallowed in the waves?

XXIX.

Two graves, two lives; two lives that beat as one,
Two perfect hopes that glowed, two spirits won;
  The world and they were made in sympathy.
Yet they were born to die, unknown to sin;
Two pure expressions of what might have been,
  They lived and died, but not as we.

www.ingramcontent.com/pod-product-compliance
Lightning Source LLC
Chambersburg PA
CBHW030857270326
41929CB00008B/463